The Rapture Of The Church Is God's Last End Time Event!

Roger Henri Trepanier

© 2022

This book is dedicated to all those on earth who are at this moment children of God through salvation. May the following truths be a reminder to all of us, as what we are waiting for, and what we are to do until this event occurs:

"But we do not want you to be uninformed, brethren, about those who are asleep, so that you will not grieve as do the rest who have no hope. For if we believe that Jesus died and rose again, even so God will bring with Him those who have fallen asleep in Jesus. For this we say to you by the word of the Lord, that we who are alive and remain until the coming of the Lord, will not precede those who have fallen asleep. For the Lord Himself will descend from heaven with a shout, with the voice of the archangel and with the trumpet of God, and the dead in Christ will rise first. Then we who are alive and remain will be caught up together with them in the clouds to meet the Lord in the air, and so we shall always be with the Lord. Therefore comfort one another with these words."

1 Thessalonians. 4:13-18

Titles available from Roger Henri Trepanier in The Truth Seeker's Library™ series:

Titles available from Roger Henri Trepanier in The Practical Helps Library™ series:

Learning to Overcome The Perplexities Of This Present Life
So, I Hear You Want To Work With Seniors?
I Will Not Have This Man To Rule Over Me!
Spiritual Truth To Warm The Heart!
Fasten Your Seatbelts: Turbulence Ahead!
Living A Normal Christian Life In An Increasingly Abnormal World!
If You Have Jesus; You Do Not Need Drugs!
To Do God's Will Is To Have A Foretaste Of Heaven!
This World Is Ready For The Rule Of The Antichrist!
President Trump And The Q Movement Versus Satan And The DEEP STATE
More Of God's Great Promises For Comfort And Encouragement!
Alert! The C-Virus Pandemic Was Satan's Practice Run For A New World Order
The Days Are Evil! The Time Is Short! Be Saved From This Perverse Generation!
Your Worldview Determines Your Wellbeing And Eternal Destiny!
What We Are Watching Is The Spirit Of The Antichrist At Work!
A Sure Cure For Loneliness!
Will God Allow President Trump To Regain The White House?

Titles available from Roger Henri Trepanier in The Christian Fiction Library™ series:

The Beginning Of A New Dawn
It Is Never Too Late For Love!
The True To Life Musings Of Fred And Ernie
Between A Rock And A Hard Place!
Love Knows No Boundaries!
A Woman Worth Pursuing!
Love Is More Than Just A Four Letter Word!
The Twists And Turns Of The Life Of Faith!

Titles available from Roger Henri Trepanier in The Word Of God Library™ series:

God's First Letter To The Thessalonians
God's Second Letter To The Thessalonians
God's Letter To Believers Through Jude
God's Three Short Letters To Believers Through John
God's Letter To Scattered Believers Through James
God's Letter To Titus
God's Prophetic Word To Mankind Through Daniel
God's Letter To Philemon And God's Letter To The Colossians
God's Consummation Of All In The Book Of Revelation
God's Letter To The Philippians
God's First Letter Through Peter
God's Second Letter Through Peter
Jonah, God's Reluctant Prophet!
God's Letter To The Galatians
God's Providence In The Book Of Esther
God's Love For Gentiles In The Book Of Ruth
God's Letter To The Ephesians
God's First Letter To Timothy
God's Second Letter To Timothy
Jesus' Sermon On The Mount: Matthews 5 to 7
Jesus" Parting Words Of Love To His Own: John 13 To 16
God's Letter To The Romans Through The Apostle Paul

INTRODUCTION

What this book deals with is the event that believers throughout the world are waiting for! When God's Son, The Lord Jesus Christ, was on earth at His first coming from Heaven to earth, He promised all those who at that time had believed in Him for salvation that He would be leaving this earth through His death at the cross, His burial, His resurrection from the dead the third day, in His ascension back to His Father in Heaven, and that HE WOULD BE COMING AGAIN! Let us note what He told the Twelve apostles the evening before He went to the cross, which is recorded for us at John 14:1-3, "[1] Do not let your heart be troubled; believe in God (The Father), believe also in Me (His Son). [2] In My Father's house (speaking of Heaven) are many dwelling places; if it were not so, I would have told you; for I go to prepare a place for you. [3] If I go and prepare a place for you, I WILL COME AGAIN AND RECEIVE YOU TO MYSELF, THAT WHERE I AM YOU MAY BE ALSO."

This "coming again" that God's Son promised His followers is the theme that we will be examining in detail in this very important and timely book, as this is an event which could occur at any moment! This is therefore an important topic for those who have a personal relationship with God, as in the pages which follow, there is much truth presented about this end time event that should encourage the hearts of every believer!

Then we are to also note that there is an Addenda at the back of the book with three sections. At Addendum A, there is a brief outline of the four ages of time, for any reading the book who might not be familiar with this information. At Addendum B, there is a brief outline of the two comings from Heaven to earth in time of God's Son, The Lord Jesus Christ, for any who may not be familiar with this information either. At Addendum C, we have a detailed look at God's resurrection program through the four ages of time relating to both believers and unbelievers. Then at Addendum D, we have a very important detailed look at God's new creation in time! And then at Addendum E, we have a presentation of the gospel, which is the good news that God has given in His word regarding His Son, The Lord Jesus Christ, for any reader who might not as yet have this vital personal relationship with God through faith in His Son.

What should also be mentioned before closing this Introduction, because we are all somewhat curious by nature, is that after completing 21 years of formal education and then spending almost 28 years working in Project Engineering and Management in the Corporate offices of two large utilities, God called His servant as a non-denominational evangelist in early 1999, and then sent him out over two thousand miles, away from family and friends, to the place of service God assigned, which is where His servant has been, and is still serving Him, as evangelist, author, and counselor. The author is a widower with three adopted children, all now married with a family of their own.

Please note the two websites listed below, which have been established for the purpose of interacting with readers and for gospel ministry:

http://www.pilgrimpathwaypublications.com

http://servantofmosthigh.com

And now my prayer is that God will richly bless you as you read this book, and greatly minister to every need in your life, as only God can! To Him be all praise, honor, and glory, with thanksgiving, both now and forevermore! Amen.

CONTENTS

CHAPTER ONE

A definition of terms, so that we might all be aware of what the subject matter of this book is!

As we begin this most important and timely book, we will first of all start by defining the terms that are found as part of the title of this book, such as "rapture," "church," and "end time," in order that we might all be aware of what the subject matter of this book will be!

What is meant by "the rapture"

While the word "rapture" itself is not found in God's word, which is the Bible; nevertheless, the truth which the term relates to definitely is found in God's word! The word "rapture" is being used in this book simply because it is the most commonly accepted word among believers for the event that is being referred to. And this event is that all the believers of the present third age of time will suddenly be taken up to meet God's Son just above the earth, to then enter God The Father's Presence in Heaven, all at the same time, both those who have experienced a physical death already, and those who are still alive physically, with this event occurring at the first stage of the second coming from Heaven to earth of God's Son, The Lord Jesus Christ!

The PRIMARY Biblical text relating to the rapture of the church is found at 1 Thessalonians 4:14-17, where God tells believers of the present third age of time, *"[14] For if we* believe that Jesus died and rose again, even so God will bring with Him those who have fallen asleep in Jesus. [15] For this we say to you by the word of the Lord, that we who are alive and remain until the coming of the Lord, will not precede those who have fallen asleep. [16] For the Lord Himself will descend from heaven with a shout, with the voice of the archangel and with the trumpet of God, and THE DEAD IN CHRIST WILL RISE FIRST. [17] THEN WE WHO ARE ALIVE AND REMAIN WILL BE CAUGHT UP TOGETHER WITH THEM TO MEET THE LORD IN THE AIR, and so we shall always be with the Lord."

A second PRIMARY text of God's word also relating to the rapture of the church is what God tells us at 1 Corinthians 15:35,42-50, "[35] But someone will say, "How are the dead raised? And with what kind of body do they come?.. [42] So also is the resurrection of the dead. It is sown a perishable body, it is raised an imperishable body; [43] it is sown in dishonor, it is raised in glory; it is sown in weakness, it is raised in power; [44] it is sown a natural body, it is raised a spiritual body. If there is a natural body, there is also a spiritual body. [45] So also it is written, "The first man, Adam, became a living soul." The last Adam became a life-giving spirit. [46] However, the spiritual is not first, but the natural; then the spiritual. [47] The first man is from the earth, earthy; the second man is from heaven. [48] As is the earthy, so also are those who are earthy; and as is the heavenly, so also are those who are heavenly. [49] Just as we have borne the image of the earthy, we will also bear the image of the heavenly. [50] Now I say this, brethren, that flesh and blood cannot inherit the kingdom of God; nor does the perishable inherit the imperishable."

A third PRIMARY text of God's word also relating to the rapture of the church is what God also tells us at John 14:1-3, where we read, "[1] "Do not let your heart be troubled; believe in God, believe also in Me. [2] In My Father's house are many dwelling places; if it were not so, I would have told you; for I go to prepare a place for you. [3] If I go and prepare a place for you, I will come again and receive you to Myself, that where I am, there you may be also."

Then a fourth PRIMARY text of God's word also relating to the rapture of the church is what God tells us at 2 Thessalonians 2:1, where we read, *"Now we request you, brethren, with regard TO THE COMING OF OUR LORD JESUS CHRIST AND OUR GATHERING TOGETHER TO HIM..."*

A fifth PRIMARY text of God's word relating to this same event is what God tells us at 2 Thessalonians 2:6,7, where we read, *"[6] And you know what restrains him now, so that in his time he will be revealed. [7] For the mystery of lawlessness is already at work; only he who now restrains will do so until he is taken out of the way."*

Then a sixth PRIMARY text of God's word relating to the rapture of the church is what God also tells us at Romans 11:25, where we read, *"For I do not want you, brethren, to be uninformed of this mystery — so that you will not be wise in your own estimation — that a partial hardening has happened to Israel UNTIL THE FULLNESS OF THE GENTILES HAS COME IN..."*

And then a seventh PRIMARY text of God's word relating to this event is what we read at Revelation 4:1,2, *"[1] After these things I looked, and behold, A DOOR STANDING OPEN IN HEAVEN, and the first voice which I had heard, like the sound of a trumpet speaking with me, said, "COME UP HERE, and I will show you what must take place after these things." [2] IMMEDIATELY I WAS IN THE SPIRIT; AND BEHOLD, A THRONE WAS STANDING IN HEAVEN, and One sitting on the throne."*

Then looking at some SECONDARY texts of God's word, where the rapture is only partially in view, but still very important to look at, let us note first what we read at Ephesians 5:27, where we read, adding verses 25 and 26 for context, *"[25] Husbands, love your wives, just as Christ also loved the church and gave Himself up for her, [26] so that He might sanctify her, having cleansed her by the washing of water with the word, [27] THAT HE MIGHT PRESENT TO HIMSELF THE CHURCH IN ALL HER GLORY, HAVING NO*

SPOT OR WRINKLE OR ANY SUCH THING; BUT THAT SHE WOULD BE HOLY AND BLAMELESS."

Then a second SECONDARY text that we need to note here is at Philippians 3:20,21, where we read, *"[20] For our citizenship is in heaven, from which also WE EAGERLY WAIT FOR A SAVIOR, THE LORD JESUS CHRIST; [21] WHO WILL TRANSFORM THE BODY OF OUR HUMBLE STATE INTO CONFORMITY WITH THE BODY OF HIS GLORY, BY THE EXERTION OF THE POWER THAT HE HAS even to subject all things to Himself."*

A third SECONDARY text of God's word, where the rapture is again partially in view, is at 1 Thessalonians 1:10, adding verse 9 for context, *"[9] For they themselves report about us what kind of a reception we had with you, and how you turned to God from idols to serve a living and true God, [10] AND TO WAIT FOR HIS SON FROM HEAVEN, whom He raised from the dead, THAT IS JESUS, WHO RESCUES US FROM THE WRATH TO COME."*

Then a fourth SECONDARY text of God's word where the rapture of the church is partially in view is at 1 Thessalonians 2:19, where we read, adding verse 20 for context, *"[19]"For who is our hope or joy or crown of exultation? Is it not even you, IN THE PRESENCE OF OUR LORD JESUS AT HIS COMING? [20] For you are our glory and joy."*

Then a fifth SECONDARY text of God's word, where the rapture is again partially in view, is at 1 Thessalonians 3:13, adding verses 11 and 12 for context, *"[11] Now may our God and Father Himself and Jesus our Lord direct our way to you; [12] and may the Lord cause you to increase and abound in love for one another, and for all people, just as we also do for you; [13] so that He may establish your hearts without blame in holiness before our God and Father AT THE COMING OF OUR LORD JESUS WITH ALL HIS SAINTS."*

And then a sixth SECONDARY text of God's word where the same event is also in view is at 1 John 3:2,3, where God says to us, *"[2] Beloved, now we are children of God, and it has not appeared as yet what we will be. We know that WHEN*

HE APPEARS, WE WILL BE LIKE HIM, BECAUSE WE WILL SEE HIM JUST AS HE IS. [3] and everyone who has this hope fixed on Him purifies himself, just as He is pure."

In the chapters which immediately follow, we will be taking a detailed look at each of the above seven primary and six secondary texts of God's word dealing with the rapture of the church. And please keep in mind that there are many other secondary texts that could also have been included here, but were not due to the fact that those chosen above will give readers a good grasp of the truth being presented. Some of these secondary texts that could have been included, but were not, are: 1 Corinthians 4:5; 1 Thessalonians 5:23; 1 Timothy 6:14; 2 Timothy 4:8; Titus 2:13; Hebrews 9:28; 10:37; 1 Peter 5:4; 1 John 2:28; Jude 1:24; and Revelation 3:3.

What is meant by "the church"

Unlike the word "rapture" – which only has the concept appear in God's word, and not the word itself – the word "church" definitely is found in God's word, with God providing a very clear definition of this term! What one will find in God's word is that God regards A LOCAL CHURCH, as not ever referring to a building, but rather as always being ALL THE BELIEVERS in a locality, whether that be a village, a town, or a city, or simply a district in any country anywhere on earth. Then all the believers ON EARTH TOGETHER form Gods UNIVERSAL CHURCH!

Let us note to begin two primary texts of God's word, where God mentions all the believers as being His church, with the first being at Ephesians 1:18-23, where we read, "[18] I pray that the eyes of your heart may be enlightened, so that you will know what is the hope of His calling, what are the riches of the glory of His inheritance in the saints, [19] and what is the surpassing greatness of His power toward us who believe. These are in accordance with the working of the strength of His might [20] which He brought about in Christ, when He raised Him from the dead and seated Him at His right hand in the heavenly places, [21] far above all rule and authority and power and dominion, and every name that is named, not only in this age but also in the one to come. [22] And He put all things in subjection under His feet, AND GAVE HIM AS HEAD OVER ALL THINGS TO THE CHURCH, [23] WHICH IS HIS BODY, the fullness of Him who fills all in all."

What God just revealed in the verses just quoted above is that during the present third age of time His Son, The Lord Jesus Christ, is now ascended back to Heaven again, being now at the right hand of His Father, where He was before He came to earth at His first coming from Heaven to take on the body in the womb of the virgin, which God The Father had prepared for Him. And as now in Heaven, God's Son is the Head of the church on earth, which God refers to as "His body" here.

Now let us look at a second passage, which is 1 Corinthians 12:12,13,27, where God reveals that it is all the believers of earth, which He regards as Christ's body on earth, "[12] For even as the body is one and yet has many members, and all the members of the body, though they are many, are one body, SO ALSO IS CHRIST. [13] FOR BY ONE (Holy) SPIRIT WE WERE ALL BAPTIZED INTO ONE BODY, whether Jews or Greeks, whether slaves or free, and we were all made to drink of one (Holy) Spirit... [27] NOW YOU (all believers of earth in this present third age of time, whether dead or alive) ARE CHRIST'S BODY, AND INDIVIDUALLY MEMBERS OF IT."

As we see from the above, God starts at verse 12 by pointing us to our own physical body on earth, which has many members, such as hands, feet, ears, and so forth, and yet is one body; and then at verse 13 with verse 27, He makes the comparison that in the same way "Christ's body" on earth is also made up of many members, which is every believer on earth!

God also shows at verse 13 above 'how' one becomes part of that one body of Christ on earth, which we have seen from Ephesians 1:22,23 quoted above is "the church," that being at the moment of one's salvation, when one undergoes a spiritual baptism, that is, an immersion which takes place, which is when God's Holy Spirit comes to indwell in one's human spirit at the moment one comes to believe the gospel, that is, God's good news relating to His Son, thereby now being spiritually united by The Holy Spirit to God's Son in Heaven and to one another on earth, to form that one body of Christ on earth!

Now let us look at some examples from God's word, which will solidify the truth of what has just been said above, first of all noting what we read at Acts 14:26, 27, "[26] From there they sailed TO ANTIOCH, from which they had been commended to the grace of God for the work that they had accomplished. [27] When they had arrived AND GATHERED THE CHURCH TOGETHER, they began to report all things that God had done with them and how He had opened a door of faith to the Gentiles." Here we see the apostle Paul and those with him returning to the city of Antioch in Syria, where we see that "the church" consisted of all the believers there!

Let us note another example of a local church consisting of all the believers in that locality, which is at 1 Corinthians 1:2, where we read, "TO THE CHURCH OF GOD WHICH IS AT CORINTH, to those who have been sanctified in Christ Jesus, saints by calling, with all who in every place call on the name of our Lord Jesus Christ, their Lord and ours..." It is clear from what we read here that the church of God in the city of Corinth in Greece consisted of all the believers in that city!

God goes on here to tell us who He is referring to as "the church of God," when He mentions that it is all those who have been set apart by God to carry out His will in that city, as those who have been cleansed of all sins and now call, with believers everywhere, on the Name of God's Son in addressing God The Father in Heaven, since becoming believers by God's calling of them to salvation!

And now, let us note a third example of a local church as all the believers in a locality, noting here what we read at 1 Corinthians 11:18, "For, in the first place, WHEN YOU COME TOGETHER AS A CHURCH, I hear that divisions exist among you; and in part I believe it." God is here again speaking to the believers of that same local church in the city of Corinth in ancient Greece, and it is clear that when the believers gather together for worship, it is the church that is gathering together!

Now let us note one example of where God speaks of all believers in every locality on earth being HIS UNIVERSAL CHURCH, which is at 1 Timothy 3:15, adding verse 14 for context, "[14] I am writing these things to you, hoping to come to you before long; [15] but in case I am delayed, I write so that you will know how one ought to conduct himself in THE HOUSEHOLD OF GOD (as where God Father indwells through His Son by The Holy Spirit), WHICH IS THE CHURCH OF THE LIVING GOD, the pillar and support of the truth."

What is meant by "end time"

What we mean by "end time" in the title and in the book is simply the end of the present third age of time. Another term which could have been used instead would have been "last days," but then that too would have required some explanation, as each of the four ages of time have 'last days' before each of these ages end. It is therefore important to keep in mind that when it is stated that the rapture of the church is God's last end time event, it is simply meant that this is the last event to occur in the present third age of time before it this present age officially comes to end and another age begins, which in this case will simply be a resuming of the second age of time in order to complete the last seven years remaining of it!

CHAPTER TWO

A detailed look at 1 Thessalonians 4:13-18, as the first primary and most important text of God's word relating to the rapture of the church!

As we look at this most important passage relating to the rapture of the church, please be aware that since not all readers of this book will be at the same place spiritually, then certain statements of truth will either need clarification, explanation, or background information, which will be provided, not only in the primary text we will be looking at in this chapter, but also in the rest of the book, as a help to the reader!

And so, we see that God begins this important passage of His word by saying through the apostle Paul at 1 Thessalonians 4:13, *"But we do not want you to be uninformed, brethren, about those who are asleep, so that you will not grieve as do the rest who have no hope."* What God is in effect saying to begin with here is that He does not want those who are believers to be without knowledge regarding those believers among them who had experienced physical death already, with God referring to those who had died as being "those who are asleep." And the reason that God regards these believers as being merely asleep here is because TO GOD DEATH IS JUST A TEMPORARY STEP UNTIL THE TIME OF RESURRECTION COMES!

We see an example of this at John 11, where Lazarus had died, who was the brother of Martha and Mary, and also one whom God's Son loved. So when The Lord Jesus was told of Lazarus' death, please note what He replied at John 11:11, "…He said to them, "Our friend Lazarus has fallen asleep; but I go, so that I may awaken him out of sleep."" And the reason that God's Son called Lazarus' physical death as "sleep" here is because He knew this was a God-appointed situation in which He would be raising Lazarus from the dead again, as we see occur at John 11:38-44. This is also why God refers to physical death as sleep also at 1 Thessalonians 4:13, because He knows that all believers, who have experienced physical death, will also be raised from the dead, when their part in THE FIRST RESURRECTION comes!

And for those who might not be too clear on this subject of God's resurrection program in time, it is important to grasp that God has TWO SEPARATE RESURRECTIONS in view in time, one resurrection being for all believers of all ages of time, and also a resurrection relating to all unbelievers of all ages of time, noting for instance Acts 24:15, where God mentions these two resurrections, "having a hope in God, which these men cherish themselves, that THERE SHALL CERTAINLY BE A RESURRECTION OF BOTH THE RIGHTEOUS AND THE WICKED."

What is also important to remember about these two resurrections is that the one relating to believers is called THE FIRST RESURRECTION (noting Revelation 20:6), which is IN FOUR STAGES, which simply means that there is a resurrection from the dead taking place at the end of each of the four ages of time, in which the believers of that age are resurrected from the dead by God. Then the resurrection relating to the unbelievers of time takes place at the last judgment of God, which is as we see at Revelation 20:11-15, where all the unbelievers of the four ages of time are raised from the dead by God all at the same time to face Him in this time of judgment, before being cast in the lake of fire and away from His Presence forever. The reader may want to read Addendum C at this point, where God's resurrection program of time is dealt with in detail, before resuming here.

And so we see at verse 4:13 here that God wants all believers on earth during the present third age to be aware of what takes place after one's present life on earth has ended, with His then giving one reason here for doing so, "so that you will not grieve as do the rest who have no hope." The word "grieve" here simply means 'to make sorrowful, to affect with sadness, cause grief.'

Because believers have a hope resting on God's promises contained in God's word, as for example noting what we read at 1 Peter 1:3,4 in this regard, "[3] Blessed be the God and Father of our Lord Jesus Christ, who according to His great mercy has caused us to be born again TO A LIVING HOPE THROUGH THE RESURRECTION OF JESUS CHRIST FROM THE DEATH, [4] TO OBTAIN AN INHERITANCE which is imperishable and undefiled and will not fade away, RESERVED IN HEAVEN FOR YOU..." And so the believer's hope rests on the fact of their being, and in their having, that life past the grave, which is based on the fact that since God's Son was raised from the dead and is now alive forevermore, then this too is what awaits every believer of all ages of time!

And so, that is why believers "will not grieve" when physical death comes, as unbelievers will, who do not have such a hope! What this means here is that when God mentions "the rest who have no hope" here, He is of course referring to the unbelievers of this world, who have no hope beyond this life, in the sense that the resurrection of God's precious Son, The Lord Jesus Christ, does not mean a resurrection to life with God for them, as it does for believers of time; but rather, for all unbelievers of time all they can expect past the grave is a resurrection of judgment leading to eternal death, that is, eternal separation from God in hell, noting what God tells us here at John 5:28,29, "[28] Do not marvel at this; for an hour is coming, in which ALL who are in the tombs will hear His voice, [29] and will come forth; those who did the good deeds (that is, believers) to a resurrection of life, those who committed the evil deeds (that is, unbelievers) to a resurrection of judgment."

Believers can look at physical death and beyond, not only without grief at that prospect, but also without fear! For it is important to see here that the fear of death and beyond is one of the things that the devil keeps unbelievers in bondage to himself by, noting for instance what God tells us at Hebrews 2:14,15, "[14] Therefore, since the children share in flesh and blood, He Himself (speaking of course of God's precious Son, The Lord Jesus Christ here) likewise also partook of the same, that through death (His own death at the cross on behalf of sinful human race) He might render powerless him who had the power of death, that is, the devil, [15] and might free those (that is, believers) who through fear of death (when yet unbelievers) were subject to slavery all their lives." Since unbelievers of time do not come to believe that God's Son came to die for their sins personally, then they will spend eternity in hell, away from the Presence of God, paying the just penalty for their own sins. And so, death in general, and that prospect in particular of what happens after death, is a cause for grief only for the unbelievers of time.

As God continues at 1 Thessalonians 4:14, He now says to us, as believers of the present third age of time, *"For if we believe that Jesus died and rose again, even so God will bring with Him those who have fallen asleep in Jesus."* What God is saying in effect here is that since believers believe that God's Son, The Lord Jesus Christ, did indeed experience a physical death at the cross, which was as payment for the sins of the whole human race, and then after being buried was indeed raised from the dead the third day, then it is just as certain that when He comes from Heaven to earth again – which will now be at the first stage of His second coming – those believers of the present third age, who will have experienced physical death prior to His coming, will indeed be returning with Him!

It is very important to grasp here that when God says, "will bring with Him those who have fallen asleep in Jesus," He is only speaking of the HUMAN SPIRIT of those believers who have died physically now being brought back from Heaven with The Lord Jesus Christ at that first stage of His second coming! For what we need to remember here is that man was constituted as being made up of three parts by God at the original creation, as we see at Genesis 2:7, "Then the Lord God formed man of dust from the ground (a human body), and breathed into his nostrils the breath of life (a human spirit); and man became a living being" (that is, a living soul), and as is also clear from what God says at 1 Thessalonians 5:23, where we read, "Now may the God of peace Himself sanctify you entirely; and may your SPIRIT AND SOUL AND BODY be preserved complete, without blame at the coming of our Lord Jesus Christ" (which is the very event that we are here looking at).

And what is important to grasp and remember about these three constituent parts of every human being is that only the body, which is the shell that encloses the spirit and the soul, ever experiences a physical death! What this means then is that the human spirit and the human soul, which are immaterial and invisible, go on to live eternally after coming into being, as when a human being is born physically on earth!

What is also important to grasp and remember here is that the human spirit was given to us by God at the original creation in order that we might commune with God, Who is a spirit Being (noting John 4:24, inhabiting a spiritual realm); and with God having constituted every human being as a living soul – that is, a person with a mind, a will, a conscience, and emotions – simply so that we might be able to commune with all other human beings, who all likewise have a soul.

And so, when a believer of this present third age dies physically, the human body is buried in a grave in the ground (at least that is the Biblical intention, further noting here that cremation is NOT of God); the human spirit at that very moment goes to God The Father in Heaven by The Holy Spirit; while the soul goes to a place below the surface of this earth, which God has called "Hades" in His word (with the word "Sheol" being the same place in view in the Old Testament).

What is being said here is critical to know and grasp for a full and proper understanding of all that we will be talking about here at 1 Thessalonians 4:14-17, and also in the rest of the book. And so, let us be clear that at the moment of physical death, the three constituent parts of a human being go to different locations in time and space of God's creation, and until such time as one's part in the first resurrection occurs, speaking of believers here!

As already mentioned above, at physical death, a believer's body goes to the grave to be buried, not cremated, due to the fact that in God's word, fire speaks of judgment on unbelievers of time, which results in their ending in the lake of fire, which is eternal hell. Since this is so, then believers should always have the body buried should physical death occur.

However, since the spirit is immaterial and invisible, as where God's Holy Spirit dwells in a believer after one becomes a child of God in salvation and while one is alive physically, that is why that human spirit goes directly to Heaven by means of The Holy Spirit at the moment a believer experiences physical death. And here, we can also note what God further tells us at Luke 8:54,55, as what happened to a physically dead girl when The Lord Jesus Christ raised her from the dead again, "[54] He, however, took her by the hand and called, saying, "Child, arise!" [55] And HER SPIRIT (human) RETURNED, and she got up immediately; and He gave orders for something to be given her to eat."

And then, as to the soul of believers, at physical death it goes to the compartment for the souls of believers in Hades, which is under the present earth, noting here what David said about his hope of life past the grave at Acts 2:26,27 in part, "[26]...Moreover my flesh also will live in hope; [27] because You will not abandon my soul to Hades..." And the reason that the soul goes to Hades is due to the fact that soul still has the sinful nature that all human beings have inherited from Adam, and which is activated at the age of accountability – which is when as a young child one first comes to know good from evil for the first time, and once one

24

chooses the evil thereby personally sinning against God for the first time – with that sinful nature not being removed from a believer's soul until one's part in the first resurrection occurs, since this is when that sinful nature is removed by God, with one then entering Heaven as blameless, without sin and without even that taint of sin!

To more properly understand what happens to believers at physical death, it would be beneficial for us to take a moment here to look at what occurred to God's Son, The Lord Jesus Christ, when He incurred physical death on our behalf, since He is our Pattern for what will happen to our body, soul, and spirit after physical death also!

First then, we note what God tells us at Luke 23:46, "And Jesus, crying out with a loud voice, said, "Father, INTO YOUR HANDS I COMMIT MY SPIRIT." Having said this, He breathed His last." We note here that the first thing which happened when The precious Lord Jesus died physically on our behalf is that His human spirit went to be with His precious Father in Heaven, as brought there by The precious Holy Spirit, noting what God also tells us at Hebrews 9:14, "how much more will the blood of Christ, WHO THROUGH THE ETERNAL SPIRIT OFFERED HIMSELF WITHOUT BLEMISH TO GOD (at the moment that He died physically and gave up His human spirit, as we have just seen at Luke 23:46), cleanse your conscience from dead works to serve the living God?"

Then secondly, we need to note what God tells us at Acts 2:31, "he (David) looked ahead and spoke of the resurrection of the Christ, that HE WAS NEITHER ABANDONED TO HADES, NOR DID His flesh SUFFER DECAY." Therefore, from this we learn that from the time that The Lord Jesus Christ died physically, His human spirit went to be with His Father in Heaven, while His human soul went to Hades, to the compartment reserved for the souls of believers of time, with this only being until His resurrection from the dead on the third day!

And then thirdly, we further need to note what God tells us at Matthew 27:58-60, where we read, "[58] This man went to Pilate and asked for the body of Jesus. Then Pilate ordered it to be given *to him.* [59] And Joseph TOOK THE BODY and wrapped it in a clean linen cloth, [60] AND LAID IT IN HIS OWN NEW TOMB, which he had hewn out in the rock; and he rolled a large stone against the entrance of the tomb and went away." Here we see that while The Lord Jesus' human spirit went to His Father in Heaven, and His soul went to the compartment reserved for the soul of believers in Hades, that His physical body went to the tomb, just outside the city gate of Jerusalem!

And then when the third day occurred, which is the day The Lord Jesus Christ was raised from the dead by His Father, then His human spirit returned from Heaven to that physically dead body still in the tomb, as did His human soul from Hades, and then He arose from the grave with a transformed visible spiritual body, now fitted to last eternity without ever again being subject to physical death; but with the same human spirit and soul, which is what characterizes one as a human being. He of course did not stop being, by His resurrection from the dead, The Son of God and still fully human in one Person, which He will remain as such for all time and eternity to come!

Therefore, at 1 Thessalonians 4:13,14 here, we have believers of the present third age primarily in view, who will have died physically, and who at the time of their part in the first resurrection, when The Lord Jesus Christ will come from Heaven to earth, as part of the first stage of His second coming, then the human spirit of these believers will return to earth with The Lord Jesus Christ to re-enter their physically dead bodies, while their human soul returns from Hades, and so they too will now experience the same resurrection from the dead that The Lord Jesus Christ experienced as the first fruit of that first resurrection! The time of their glorification would have now come when the sinful nature is removed and one's body is changed to a spiritual body to last forever in God's Presence!

As to the truth of that human body being raised a spiritual body at the time that one's part in the first resurrection comes, this is a truth that God makes known at 1 Corinthians

15:42-49, which we would benefit from noting at this point, where we read, with some comments added in brackets as a help, "[42] So also is the resurrection of the dead. It is sown a perishable body (at physical death), it is raised an imperishable body; [43] it is sown in dishonor, it is raised in glory; it is sown in weakness, it is raised in power; [44] it is sown a natural body (in death), it is raised a spiritual body (at the time of one's part in the first resurrection). If there is a natural body, there is also a spiritual body. [45] So also it is written, "The first man, Adam, became a living soul." The last Adam (God's Son) became a life-giving spirit. [46] However, the spiritual is not first, but the natural (at the time of one's physical birth into this present world); then the spiritual (at the time of one's part in the first resurrection). [47] The first man (Adam) is from the earth, earthy; the second man (The Lord Jesus Christ, at His first coming to earth) is from heaven. [48] As is the earthy, so also are those who are earthy; and as is the heavenly, so also are those who are heavenly. [49] Just as we have borne the image of the earthy (at the moment of our physical birth into this world), we will also bear the image of the heavenly (when as believers we receive our new spiritual body at the time of our part in the first resurrection)!

In having now informed believers about what happens to those believers who would have died physically, here termed "those who have fallen asleep in Jesus," the apostle Paul is then led of God at 1 Thessalonians 4:15 to now speak of those believers who will still be alive physically when God's Son, The Lord Jesus Christ returns for all believers of the present third age, noting now what we there read, *"For this we say to you by the word of the Lord, that we who are alive and remain until the coming of the Lord, will not precede those who have fallen asleep."*

And so the further truth to be grasped here is that when God's Son, The Lord Jesus Christ, returns to just above the earth at the first stage of His second coming from Heaven at the end of the present third age, those "who are alive and remain until the coming of The Lord" – which speaks of those believers, who are on earth and have never died physically – they "will not precede those who have fallen asleep," meaning that they will not experience the receiving from God of their new visible, eternal, and spiritual bodies until those who have died physically during the present age, have received theirs! So we see an order here in the way God proceeds to give believers of the present third age their new spiritual bodies, in that those who have died are first raised from the dead, then only along with them do believers of the present age, who are still alive physically, then receive their new visible, eternal and spiritual bodies!

Then at 1 Thessalonians 4:16,17, the apostle Paul is led of God to repeat the truth already just disclosed, now also adding further details, for truth such as this bears repeating since it is not something a believer would ever think of, nor reason out for oneself, of what God has already made known! And so God continues and now further says, *"[16] For the Lord Himself will descend from heaven with a shout, with the voice of the archangel and with the trumpet of God, and the dead in Christ will rise first. [17] Then we who are alive and remain will be caught up together with them in the clouds to meet the Lord in the air, and so we shall always be with the Lord."*

When we read here at verse 4:16, "For the Lord Himself will descend from heaven," we are to realize that this is speaking of God's Son, The Lord Jesus Christ, as Who is here in view, which, as already mentioned, is now at the first stage of His second coming from Heaven, which is at the end of the present third age.

And so "The Lord Himself will descend from Heaven," which as we see from 1 Thessalonians 4:17 here is "in the clouds... in the air," just above the present earth, which is in contrast to the second stage of The Lord Jesus' second coming being actually to the earth, which coming only occurs at the end of the seven years of God's judgments coming on the unbelievers of this world, which is during the last seven years remaining of the second age of time.

That this is so is something that is clear from Daniel's prophecy of Daniel 9:24-27, and also from what God tells us at Zechariah 4:14, where we read in part, "In that day (that is,

28

at the time of the second stage of His second coming at the end of the seven years of God's time of judgment) His feet will stand on the Mount of Olives, which is in front of Jerusalem on the east...," and also from what God tells us at Acts 1:9-11, "[9] And after He (The Lord Jesus Christ) had said these things, He was lifted up (from the Mount of Olives) while they were looking on, and a cloud received Him out of their sight. [10] And as they were gazing intently into the sky while He was going, behold, two men in white clothing stood beside them. [11] They also said, "Men of Galilee, why do you stand looking into the sky? This Jesus, who has been taken up from you into heaven (at the time of ascension at His first coming to earth), will come in just the same way as you have watched Him go into heaven."

At both Zechariah 4:14 and Acts 1:11 here, we have The Son of God, The Lord Jesus Christ, prophesied as coming again to the very place He ascended into Heaven from, that being from the Mount of Olives, just east of Jerusalem in Israel, at the second stage of His second coming, which is at the end of the seven years remaining of the second age of time (noting Revelation 19:11-21)!

But here at 1 Thessalonians 4:16, when The Lord Jesus Himself will descend from Heaven, and will remain in the clouds just above the earth, at that very moment it will be, "with a shout, with the voice of the archangel and with the trumpet of God, and the dead in Christ will rise first." The questions which arise here are: Why a shout; why the voice of the archangel; and why the trumpet of God? Are they all for the purpose of calling the dead bodies in Christ, relating to the present third age, to now arise from the dead?

The word "shout" here means 'a call, a summons, a shout of command.' Two very important verses in this regard are John 5:28,29, which we already quoted, but which we need to note again here for our present purpose, "[28] Do not marvel at this; for an hour is coming, in which all who are in the tombs WILL HEAR HIS VOICE, [29] AND WILL COME FORTH; those who did the good deeds to a resurrection of life, those who committed the evil deeds to a resurrection of judgment."

And so here at 1 Thessalonians 4:16, we have all the believers of the present third age in view, who will have died physically, who at the coming of The Lord Jesus Christ to just above the earth at the end of the present third age, HEAR HIS VOICE IN THAT SHOUT AND COME FORTH, to have that human body in which one died, now changed to a spiritual body to last forever, while at the same time, as already described above, having the human spirit coming from Heaven with The Lord Jesus Christ, which is again united with the soul coming from the compartment of the believers in Hades, minus the sinful nature, which is now removed due to one's time of glorification having come; and with that spirit and soul now being clothed with that new spiritual body to last forever in God's Presence!

Here we can again note what God tells us at Philippians 3:20,21, which also speaks of what now takes place relating to what has just been stated above, "[20] For our citizenship is in heaven, from which also we eagerly wait for a Savior, the Lord Jesus Christ; [21] who (when He comes at the time of the first stage of His second coming) will transform the body of our humble state into conformity with the body of His glory, by the exertion of the power that He has even to subject all things to Himself."

Then the word "voice," mentioned at 1 Thessalonians 4:16, which speaks of uttered words, are here seen as coming from "the archangel." We note that the word "archangel" occurs only twice in God's word, and only in the New Testament, here at 1 Thessalonians 4:16 and also at Jude 1:9, where God says, "But Michael the archangel, when he disputed with the devil and argued about the body of Moses, did not dare pronounce against him a railing judgment, but said, "The Lord rebuke you!" " So we see from this that in the realm of created angelic beings, there is an archangel named Michael, who in rank was above the unfallen angels.

In my book, "The Mysterious World of Angels And Demons," we there saw that there is another unfallen archangel, that being Gabriel, mentioned at Luke 1:19,26. We are not told here at 1 Thessalonians 4:16 which of these two archangels it was, whether it was Michael or Gabriel, who is here in view as the one whom God The Father appoints to come and be with His Son, The Lord Jesus Christ, when He brings together the spirit and soul of physically dead believers into a new spiritual body.

So what we are to see here is that while the shout of God's Son is to bring the dead body of believer's that have died back to life again, the voice of the archangel is to direct the unfallen angels under his command to go and have the souls of believers now in the compartment of the believers in Hades be brought back to where The Lord Jesus Christ is above the earth. For what needs to be grasped here is that when these believers died physically, it was their guardian angel who brought their soul to the compartment of the believers in Hades in the first place! The spirit and the soul of a person are never free to move on their own from place to place in time and space, when not in a body, for as we have already noted, not even the human spirit goes to God in Heaven on its own, but rather The Holy Spirit is The One Who brings the human spirit to God, with The Holy Spirit now involved again with God's Son in bringing that spirit back at the time of glorification!

And so, we observe here that so far we have seen the shout of God's Son Himself going forth to summon the dead bodies of all believers of the present third age, who will have died physically up to the time of the first stage of His second coming, to now arise from the dead for their time of glorification has come. At the same time, as something that happens simultaneously, we have the voice of the archangel, who is either Michael or Gabriel, going out to the guardian angels to escort the souls of the believers in the compartment of believers in Hades, in effect telling them to now bring those souls back to their physically dead bodies of earth, with the sinful nature being removed from these souls before being united with the spirit coming with God's Son from God in Heaven, as escorted by The Holy Spirit, to now indwell the new spiritual body at this time of the glorification of all physically dead believers of the present third age!

This now leaves "the trumpet of God" mentioned here at 1 Thessalonians 4:16, for us to now determine what the meaning is. In a study of the word "trumpet" in Scripture, which was done, it was discovered that "the trumpet of God" in view here at 1 Thessalonians 4:16 referred to a trumpet sound which God The Father causes the angels to give at this time due to precious souls coming into the Presence of God, in the very same way that we see Moses bring the Israelites into God's Presence at Exodus 19:16,17, where we read, "[16] So it came about on the third day, when it was morning, that there were thunder and lightning flashes and a thick cloud upon the mountain and A VERY LOUD TRUMPET SOUND, so that all the people who were in the camp trembled. [17] And Moses BROUGHT THE PEOPLE OUT OF THE CAMP TO MEET GOD, and they stood at the foot of the mountain."

At Hebrews 12:18,19, the same verses from Exodus 19 are again in view, with God now saying to believers of the present third age of time, "[18] For you have not come to a mountain that can be touched and to a blazing fire, and to darkness and gloom and whirlwind, [19] and to the blast of a trumpet and the sound of words which sound was such that those who heard begged that no further word be spoken to them," seeing here that the equivalent of the word "trumpet" from the Old Testament is the same word "trumpet" here in the New Testament in view at 1 Thessalonians 4:16. Therefore, "the trumpet of God" is to be seen as being a trumpet-like sound that God The Father causes to be heard at this time, due to the fact that God's Son is in the process of bringing all the precious believers of the present third age into the Presence of His Father in Heaven! And let us not forget that this relates to THE RAPTURE OF THE CHURCH here!

Then after speaking of those believers of the present third age in a comprehensive statement, in terms of telling us what occurs at the time of the rapture of the church, God now goes on through the apostle Paul and completes at 1 Thessalonians 4:17 the picture for us of all that takes place during that time of rapture, by now going to speak of all those who will still be alive on earth, when The Lord Jesus Christ

32

returns at the first stage of His second coming, which is at the end of this present third age, as we now again read there, "Then we who are alive and remain will be caught up together with them in the clouds to meet the Lord in the air, and so we shall always be with the Lord."

And so we see here that, "we who are alive and remain will be caught up together with them in the clouds to meet the Lord in the air," this is clearly now referring to all the believers alive on earth at the end of the present third age, when The Lord Jesus returns again at the first stage of His second coming. As we are clearly told here, those believers who are alive physically at that time "will be caught up together with them in the clouds... in the air," which is above this present earth, as being where the believers still alive are now gathered to The Lord Jesus and also with the believers who will have died physically during the present age, now in their new spiritual bodies.

And now the same occurs in an instant, as fast as the twinkling of an eye, those believers on earth will likewise now have their physical bodies changed into spiritual bodies for all eternity, including the removal of the sinful nature as that transformation takes place, and as all these transformed believers now all rise up toward the clouds to "meet The Lord in the air," as being all those believers yet alive and making up God's church yet on earth during the present third age! This is the time of glorification of all believers of the present third age, being when all enter God's very Presence in Heaven with God's Son as their part in the first resurrection!

Then we see that the apostle Paul is led of God to add at the end of 1 Thessalonians 4:17, "and so we shall always be with The Lord," and this is good news indeed, to ever be with God, which is forever, which is why the apostle Paul is further led of God to add at 1 Thessalonians 4:18, *"Therefore comfort one another with these words."* As any believer knows, who has lived long enough on earth as a child of God – especially if one has been brought to a measure of spiritual maturity by God – there is great anticipation for the moment of our glorification as children of God yet on earth, for then we will not only be perfectly conformed to the image of God's precious Son forever, and will not only have a new spiritual body in the image of God's Son, our Lord Jesus Christ (noting Philippians 3:21 with 1 John 3:2), but we will also have our sinful nature removed from our soul, which means never ever again sinning against God from that moment on!

And a further very important truth which must be seen here, relating to what has just been noted, is that the judgment seat of Christ must be seen as having been completed by the time the first stage of The Lord Jesus Christ's second coming is completed just above the earth, where God's Son is seen gathering all the believers of the present third age to Himself, as we have seen at 1 Thessalonians 4:14-17, before we see all the believers of the present third age in Heaven. And let us remember that this 'judgment seat of Christ' is an instantaneous event, which takes place in a moment of time.

We should therefore note that God has this judgment seat of Christ in view specifically at three passages of the New Testament, first noting Romans 14:10, where we read, "But you, why do you judge your brother? Or you again, why do you regard your brother with contempt? For we (having all believers of the present third age in view here) will all stand before the judgment seat of God." Then secondly also at 2 Corinthians 5:10, where we read, "For we (again having all believers of the present third age in view here) must all appear before the judgment seat of Christ, so that each one may be recompensed for his deeds in the body, according to what he has done, whether good or bad."

And third passage that can be mentioned here is at 1 Corinthians 3:10-15, where we see that the judgment seat of Christ is simply referred to here as "the day" at verse 13, but where we learn what does take place at the judgment seat of Christ, noting now what we there read, "[10] According to the grace of God which was given to me, like a wise master builder I laid a foundation, and another is building on it. But each man must be careful how he builds on it (in reference to the days all believers of the present third age are allotted by God on earth from the time of one's salvation until the time one leaves this earth). [11] For no man can lay a foundation other than the one which is laid, which is Jesus Christ (only what God has done through His Son by The Holy Spirit in us and through us as believers will count as building on the foundation, not what believers ever do from self apart from God). [12] Now if any man builds on the foundation with gold, silver, precious stones, wood, hay, straw, [13] each man's work will become evident; for the day (in reference to the time of the judgment seat of Christ) will show it because it is to be revealed with fire, and the fire itself will test the quality of each man's work. [14] If any man's work which he has built on it remains, he will receive a reward. [15] If any man's work is burned up, he will suffer loss; but he himself will be saved, yet so as through fire."

So the point of mentioning the judgment seat of Christ here is to make us aware as believers of the present third age of time that this event occurs in a moment of time as we all stand before God's Son in the clouds above the earth, as we have seen at 1 Thessalonians 4:14-17, and just before we all make our entrance into God The Father's Presence in Heaven accompanied by God's Son, The Lord Jesus Christ, by the enablement of The Holy Spirit!

So what God has disclosed here at 1 Thessalonians 4:13-17 are all indeed words of truth that will bring encouragement and comfort to the life of any believer alive upon hearing this truth explained in simple terms! All praise, honor, and glory, with thanksgiving, be to God for His mercy, love, and faithfulness, in bringing all this to pass as wholly a work of His grace and power alone, and for His glory alone!

CHAPTER THREE

A detailed look at 1 Corinthians 15:35-50 as the second PRIMARY text of God's word relating to the rapture of the church

In this chapter, we will look at a second PRIMARY text of God's word also relating to the rapture of the church, which is what God says at 1 Corinthians 15:35-50, which relates specifically to the resurrection from the dead of believers of the present third age of time. What is important to grasp here is that this is ADDITIONAL INFORMATION to what God already said regarding the resurrection of believers of the present third age at 1 Thessalonians 4:14-17, since God's first letter to the Thessalonians was given to believers BEFORE God's first letter to the Corinthians!

And so, let us now look in detail at what God tells us at 1 Corinthians 15:35-50, "*[35] But someone will say, "How are the dead raised? And with what kind of body do they come?[36] You fool! That which you sow does not come to life unless it dies; [37] and that which you sow, you do not sow the body which is to be, but a bare grain, perhaps of wheat or of something else. [38] But God gives it a body just as He wished, and to each of the seeds a body of its own. [39] All flesh is not the same flesh, but there is one flesh of men, and another flesh of beasts, and another flesh of birds, and another of fish. [40] There are also heavenly bodies and earthly bodies, but the glory of the heavenly is one, and the* glory of the earthly is another. [41] There is one glory of the sun, and another glory of the moon, and another glory of the stars; for star differs from star in glory. [42] So also is the resurrection of the dead. It is sown a perishable body, it is raised an imperishable body; [43] it is sown in dishonor, it is raised in glory; it is sown in weakness, it is raised in power; [44] it is sown a natural body, it is raised a spiritual body. If there is a natural body, there is also a spiritual body. [45] So also it is written, "The first man, Adam, became a living soul." The last Adam became a life-giving spirit. [46] However, the spiritual is not first, but the natural; then the spiritual. [47] The first man is from the earth, earthy; the second man is from heaven. [48] As is the earthy, so also are those who are earthy; and as is the heavenly, so also are those who are heavenly. [49] Just as we have borne the image of the earthy, we will also bear the image of the heavenly. [50] Now I say this, brethren, that flesh and blood cannot inherit the kingdom of God; nor does the perishable inherit the imperishable."

Please note that this passage of God's word opens at verse 35 with someone asking two questions, the first being, "How are the dead raised?," meaning at the time of one's resurrection from the dead, which is in view here. And the answer here is always in relation to God's Son! In other words, what applied to the resurrection from the dead of God's Son, The Lord Jesus Christ, will also apply to the resurrection from the dead of every believer in any age of time, who experiences physical death!

And so, let us note here what God tells us at Acts 2:23,24 regarding the resurrection from the dead of God's Son, The Lord Jesus Christ, there reading, "[23] this Man, delivered over by the predetermined plan and foreknowledge of God, you nailed to a cross by the hands of godless men and PUT HIM TO DEATH. [24] BUT GOD RAISED HIM UP AGAIN putting an end to the agony of death, since it was impossible for Him to be held in its power." What this means then, in regards to the "how" the dead are raised in time, the answer is that IT IS ALWAYS BY THE POWER OF GOD, AS A WORK THAT GOD ALONE DOES!

And then as to the second question, "with what kind of body do they come?," God now answers this question by first pointing out truths from the natural world at verses 36 to 41, before He turns to give the answer to what is now not only applicable to the body of His own dear Son, but also to the body of all human beings who happen to die physically in any age of time, and then are later raised from the dead by God in resurrection.

And so we see that at verse 36 God points out that DEATH first precedes anything that is planted in the ground. We see from John 12:24 that this was a truth that God's Son taught when foretelling His own coming death and subsequent resurrection from the dead, when He there stated, ""Truly, truly, I say to you, unless a grain of wheat falls into the earth and dies, it remains alone; but if it dies, it bears much fruit."

Then at verses 37 and 38, God goes on to point out that what is sown in the ground never looks the same when the harvest comes as what was planted in the ground, as any farmer knows. If one plants seeds for carrots, what will eventually grow out of the ground will look much different than the seeds that were planted! And as we see here, it is God Who even in the natural world is likewise responsible for how what was planted in the ground will look when it comes out of the ground!

Then God goes on at verse 39 to point out that all that exists in creation has a different outward appearance, one specie from another. And so, mankind has one appearance, beasts of the field have another, birds have another, and so too is this true for fish!

Then at verses 40 and 41, God goes on to point out that just as there are earthly bodies on earth, there are also bodies in the heavens, such as sun, moon, and stars, with all of these having a different glory, where the word "glory" here refers to the natural brightness and splendor that God gave each at the time of creation!

Then beginning at verse 42, and going to verse 50, God now takes the truth just stated at verses 36 to 41 relating to the natural world and now relates this to how He now answers the second question posed at verse 35, namely, "with what kind of body do they come," as when human beings are resurrected from the dead?

And what we will now see here is that God takes the same body which died physically, which is the body with which we enter this world, and at the time of the resurrection from the dead, God takes that body and transforms it INTO A SPIRITUAL BODY, which is no longer subject to death, which means that this body can now last forever, for whatever place that body will then end up, whether in Heaven with God, or in hell with the devil.

And so, God begins at verses 42 to point out that the body that is sown into the ground as A PERISHABLE BODY at the time of physical death, will at some point in time appointed by God be raised by God in resurrection and will then be AN IMPERISHABLE BODY!

Then God goes on to further point out at verse 43 that in physical death that human body was SOWN IN DISHONOR, in that it still had a sinful nature while the soul remained in the body, but when the soul returns to the physically dead body at the time of one's part in the first resurrection, it is now RAISED IN GLORY, since that sinful nature will now have been removed from the soul on its return, so that the resurrected body is now ready for glory, which is to enter God's Presence no longer having any taint of sin!

Then we note that God goes on and also points out at verse 43 that the physically dead human body that is buried is SOWN IN WEAKNESS, in terms of being able to age and die, but no longer can do so when raised from the dead in resurrection, for it is RAISED IN POWER, in that the body can longer age nor die!

Then we note that God finally reaches the truth at verse 44 that He wants believers specially to grasp and remember, which is that the human body that is sown in physical death is A NATURAL BODY, but is raised as A SPIRITUAL BODY in resurrection. What God means by the word "natural," here is what we were in Adam, when created with a body, spirit, and soul at original creation; in contrast to what we become in resurrection, which is with a spiritual body that now lasts forever, a soul without the sinful nature that is ready to enter God's Presence, but the same human spirit that God had imparted at the original creation (noting Genesis 2:7 quoted below)! And so God closes verse 44 by simply stating the truth that just the natural body of mankind is a reality, so too is the spiritual body that God gives in resurrection, it is also a real body that exists in both time and space!

And to amplify the truth just stated at verse 44, God now goes on at verse 45 and points out that it is written of Adam, as the first man created by God, that he "became a living soul," when God created him at the original creation, as we see at Genesis 2:7, where we read, "Then the Lord God formed man of dust from the ground (the human body), and breathed into his nostrils the breath of life (the human spirit given); and man became a living being" (that is, a living soul).

Then God goes on at verse 45 and speaks of His own dear Son, The Lord Jesus Christ, as "the last Adam," in reference to when He came from Heaven to earth at His first coming in the likeness and innocence of the first man, Adam, but Who is now in Heaven, after His resurrection from the dead, as "a life-giving spirit," meaning that He ever exists as a spiritual Being with His Father, and that it is through Him that God The Father now grants eternal life to all who believe in Him!

Let us note here what God 's Son Himself said at John 11:25, "I am the resurrection and the life; he who believes in Me will live even if he dies," and then also what we read of God's Son in resurrection at Hebrews 7:23-25, "[23] The former priests (of the nation of Israel), on the one hand, existed in greater numbers because they were prevented by death from continuing, [24] but Jesus, on the other hand, because He continues forever (in resurrection at His Father's right Hand in Heaven), holds His priesthood permanently. [25] Therefore He is able also to save forever those who draw near to God through Him, since He always lives to make intercession for them."

When God speaks of "the first man, Adam," He is making reference to the fact that this man, Adam, is the first of God's human creation on this earth, with all other human beings to come being descended from him. And in calling His Son "the last Adam," God is here indicating that while His Son came to this earth in the likeness and innocence of the first man, Adam, nevertheless, through His death, His burial, and His resurrection from the dead, He is now The Head of a new spiritual creation of God in Him, as He is the firstborn of that new creation of God! The reader may want to pause here for a moment and go to Addendum D, to there read, "God's new creation in time" before resuming to read here.

As God then continues at verse 46, He there points out that the natural body is first, then the spiritual, which was the case even for His own dear Son, The Lord Jesus Christ. All human beings first have a visible, but temporal physical body at birth into this world, consisting of body, soul, and spirit (noting 1 Thessalonians 5:23), before obtaining a still visible, but now eternal spiritual body at the time of one's part in the first resurrection!

Then God continues at verse 47 and points out that the first man, Adam, was from the earth, which God calls "earthy," due to his body having come from the dust of the ground, to which it returns at the time of physical death (noting Genesis 2:7 with 3:19). In contrast to this, "the second man," here in reference to God's Son, came from Heaven to earth to take on a human body in the likeness of the innocence of Adam as first created, and then through death, burial, and resurrection from the dead, now has a spiritual body that all human beings will one day share in resurrection, that being those who are believers, to be with Him in Heaven in that spiritual body; while all unbelievers will find themselves in hell with the devil in that spiritual body!

At verse 48, when God says, "as is the earthy," He is making reference to whom we are descended from, which is Adam, which therefore means that all those who follow in the likeness of Adam will also be earthy, and therefore subject to physical death as he was. And then God goes on and now

42

says in contrast to this, "as is the heavenly, in terms of sharing the likeness of His Son in salvation, this therefore means that all such will all one day also share the heavenly with Him in resurrection!

At verse 49, God simply amplifies the truth just stated in the second part of verse 48, namely that just as believers have born the image of Adam, the first man from the earth, in coming into this world through a physical birth; so too will all one day bear the image of the second Man from Heaven, God's Son, The Lord Jesus Christ, due to having undergone a spiritual birth leading to one's part in the first resurrection at a time appointed by God!

Then at verse 50, God simply concludes this passage, which started at verse 35, by simply stating in a summarizing statement what is now true during the present third age of time, namely that a human being in "flesh and blood," that is, having a physical body that one was born into this world with, cannot inherit the kingdom of God, that is, one cannot enter that kingdom in Heaven (noting Colossians 1:12-14), over which God's Son now rules since His ascension during the present third age of time.

So the further conclusion here by God at verse 50 is that the "perishable," in reference to human beings still in physical bodies subject to physical death, simply cannot enter the realm of the "imperishable," in reference to Heaven itself, as God's eternal and uncreated abode, in that one cannot enter that realm unless one has first come to personally know God The Father through faith in His Son, and then one has experienced one's part in the first resurrection, which is when one now gains that spiritual, and now imperishable body to now enter God's very Presence, which is forever! All praise, honor, and glory be to God, with thanksgiving, both now and forevermore! Amen.

And before we leave this present chapter, and since we are in the process of dealing with the second question posed above at verse 35, namely, "with what kind of body do they come?," we should look more deeply into that question here, and also in the statement of verse 50 above that "flesh and blood cannot inherit the kingdom of God." And so our intent here is on gaining further knowledge of what that spiritual but visible body of God's Son, The Lord Jesus Christ, consisted of after his resurrection from the dead, since that is also the same kind of spiritual and visible body that all human beings will have once one experiences one's part in the first resurrection, whether through physical death, or for some, through a translation, if still alive when that event occurs.

And one passage which we can look at here to shed some light on this is noting what God has had recorded at Luke 24:36-40, where we read, "[36] While they were telling these things, He Himself (God's Son, after His resurrection from the dead) stood in their midst and said to them, "Peace be to you." [37] But they were startled and frightened and thought that they were seeing A SPIRIT. [38] And He said to them, "Why are you troubled, and why do doubts arise in your hearts? [39] See My hands and My feet, that it is I Myself; touch Me and see, FOR A SPIRIT DOES NOT HAVE FLESH AND BONES AS YOU SEE THAT I HAVE." [40] And when He had said this, He showed them His hands and His feet."

Please keep in mind here that God's Son was here before the disciples after His resurrection from the dead, which means in His new spiritual body. And what needs to be grasped here is that He was visible to the human eye and He still looked in appearance as before, since the disciples recognized Him when He suddenly appeared in their midst.

But please also note an important truth at verse 39, where He says to them, "a spirit does not have flesh and bones as you see that I have." Therefore, it is clear that He was in a new body that was spiritual, but that body was visible, in that it was flesh and bones. There were also characteristic marks of the old body present in this transformed body, which is evident when God's Son here shows the disciples His hands and His feet, which obviously sill had the print marks from the nails by which He was nailed to the cross. Those signs will forever be with Him!

There are also other truths which we need to be observed here before we leave this very important investigation in the nature of the resurrected body of God's Son, The Lord Jesus Christ, one being what we read Hebrews 2:14 in part, "Therefore, since the children share in flesh and blood, He Himself likewise also partook of the same..." What this is saying to us is that the physical body that God's own precious Son came into this world with, as born of a virgin and without the sinful nature of Adam, was just like any other physical body, in that it was FLESH AND BLOOD. Now what is important to observe in relation to the passage at Luke 24:39 above is that there, God's Son, while in His resurrected body, could no longer say "flesh and blood," for the body was no longer physical, but was now only "flesh and bones," so as to give that new spiritual body structure so that it could be seen!

But the important truth here is that IT NO LONGER HAD BLOOD, for blood is what characterizes the life of the physical body, noting what God says at Leviticus 17:14, where we read, "For as for the life of all flesh, ITS BLOOD IS IDENTIFIED WITH ITS LIFE. Therefore I said to the sons of Israel, 'You are not to eat the blood of any flesh, FOR THE LIFE OF ALL FLESH IS ITS BLOOD; whoever eats it shall be cut off.' "

And we are then to see that it was not only blood that the new spiritual and visible body of God's Son, The Lord Jesus Christ, now was without in resurrection, for there was something else, which we learn about at 1 Corinthians 6:13 in part, where we read, "Food is for the stomach and the stomach is for food, BUT GOD WILL DO AWAY WITH BOTH OF THEM."

And the doing away with both food and the stomach, as mentioned by God here, is to be seen as relating to the resurrected body. In other words, that new resurrected body that God's Son now has in resurrection does not have a stomach, nor does it require food! We do see God's Son take a piece of broiled fish at Luke 24:42,43, however, this was done to show them that He was more than just a spirit in their midst. He did not need food to sustain that new spiritual body that was now flesh and bones since it was eternal in that state, no longer subject to aging nor death.

45

Now what we have said so far brings up yet another truth relating to the resurrection body, which is found in what God says to us at Mark 12:18-25, where we read, "[18] Some Sadducees (who say that there is no resurrection) came to Jesus, and began questioning Him, saying, [19] "Teacher, Moses wrote for us that if a man's brother dies and leaves behind a wife and leaves no child, his brother should marry the wife and raise up children to his brother. [20] There were seven brothers; and the first took a wife, and died leaving no children. [21] The second one married her, and died leaving behind no children; and the third likewise; [22] and so all seven left no children. Last of all the woman died also. [23] IN THE RESURRECTION, WHEN THEY RISE AGAIN, which one's wife will she be? For all seven had married her." [24] Jesus said to them, "Is this not the reason you are mistaken, that you do not understand the Scriptures or the power of God? [25] For WHEN THEY RISE FROM THE DEAD, THEY NEITHER MARRY NOR ARE GIVEN IN MARRIAGE, BUT ARE LIKE THE ANGELS IN HEAVEN."

Here we see that these unbelieving religious leaders of the nation of Israel thought they had God's Son stumped with this seemingly insurmountable problem, namely that seven brothers had married the same woman, so after death, whose wife would she be? And as we see here, God's Son points out to them that once one rises from the dead in resurrection, there is no longer any marriage, for one is "like the angels in heaven."

It is important to realize what is meant by this statement here, "like the angels in heaven," which is that human beings will no longer be male nor female, but will be neuter, like the angels, which are neither male nor female. There is no reproduction after one's own kind among the angels, so there is no need for reproductive organs, which further means that there is no need to differentiate the sexes, as is now the case in this present physical realm. It is to be observed that angelic beings only take on a body in making an appearance into this physical realm, which is always as a male (noting Luke 24:4 with Luke 24:22,23), never as a female angel!

46

One more important truth to look into here regarding the resurrection body of God's Son, The Lord Jesus Christ, is its age at the moment of His resurrection from the dead, which truth also affects the rest of the human race. We know from Luke 3:23 that God's Son began His public ministry at the age of thirty, and then had a three and half year public ministry before He died at the cross, was buried, and then was raised again from the dead in resurrection the third day. What this means then is that when God's Son was resurrected from the dead, He was thirty-three years old. And the significance for the whole of the human race to be raised from the dead in resurrection is that every human being so raised in resurrection will, I believe, also be thirty-three years old! Since there is no longer any aging, then this means perpetually thirty-three for all eternity!

What is also important to keep in mind in regard to what has just been stated is that when Adam and Eve were created by God at the original creation, they were created as full adults (and likely at thirty-three years of age), and not as babies! And we also need to be aware that there are no babies in Heaven. Any infant who dies before the age of accountability, which includes every fetus ever aborted by the way, will automatically be in Heaven! But when the resurrection from the dead comes, they will not be fetuses nor infants in Heaven! Similarly at the other end of the scale, there will not be any aged person in Heaven either, so no need for any more perms to keep one's hair from going white, no more false teeth, no more crutches or wheelchairs. We will all be thirty-three, whether young or old before our resurrection from the dead!

So let us keep in mind that critical truth already mentioned, which is that the resurrection from the dead of all believers of the four ages of time by God, beginning with His own precious Son, involves A NEW CREATION OF GOD, in that those human beings raised in resurrection are neither like their former selves in the physical realm, nor will they be fully like the angelic beings God already has in existence as part of the original creation. This will be a new creation, which is why we see God create a new heaven and new earth at

Revelation 21:1, which will specifically be for that new creation of God, namely all the believers of time and all the angels now with Him in Heaven!

CHAPTER FOUR

A detailed look at John 14:1-3 as the third PRIMARY text of God's word relating the rapture of the church

In this chapter we will look at a third PRIMARY text of God's word also relating to the rapture of the church, which is what God tells us at John 14:1-3, where we read, *"[1] Do not let your heart be troubled; believe in God, believe also in Me. [2] In My Father's house are many dwelling places; if it were not so, I would have told you; for I go to prepare a place for you. [3] If I go and prepare a place for you, I will come again and receive you to Myself, that where I am, there you may be also."*

We note from the above verses that God's Son now seeks to encourage the disciples – that is, the Eleven, with Judas Iscariot having now left the group, being on his way to betray Him to the leadership of the nation of Israel in unbelief – saying first of all at John 14:1, "Let not your heart be troubled; believe in God (The Father), believe also in Me" (His Son). The Lord Jesus knows that the disciple's hearts are troubled at events that have transpired, first telling them that one of them would betray Him (verse 13:21), then telling them that He would now be leaving them and they could not go with Him (verse 13:33), and even now just sharing that Peter will deny Him three times (verse 13:38). Just the prospect of being physically separated from God's Son after being together night and day for approximately three and a half years would be upsetting to the disciples!

The Lord Jesus also knows that they do not understand all that was happening and even what He had already told them. For what we need to be aware of here is that they were seeing the future in accord with what the Old Testament prophesied – which were the only Scriptures they had at that time – expecting a visible Kingdom on earth, with God's Son ruling as King, noting here for instance what God had prophesied at Daniel 2:44 regarding that coming Kingdom on earth

, "In the days of those kings the God of heaven will set up a kingdom which will never be destroyed, and that kingdom will not be left for another people; it will crush and put an end to all these kingdoms, but it will itself endure forever."

We also see from Acts 1:6, which would be after God's Son had risen from the dead and had appeared to them, and before His ascension back to Heaven, that even then they still had that earthly Kingdom on their minds, as we now there read, "So when they had come together, they were asking Him, saying, "Lord, is it at this time You are restoring the kingdom to Israel?""

These disciples knew that the Lord Jesus was The Messiah (noting Matthew 16:16), which when translated meant 'Christ' (noting John 1:41). However, what they did not fully grasp was 'why' the postponement of the establishment of the Kingdom on earth, not yet understanding from Gods' word that there would be two comings of God's Son from Heaven to earth. They were, unfortunately, not grasping the need for God's Son to first have to come as "The Lamb of God Who takes away the sin of the world" (noting John 1:29), before He could return a second time to establish that Kingdom on earth, which would now only be at the time of the second stage of His second coming!

It is in this type of atmosphere, where one's familiar day to day world was about to be turned upside down, that The precious Lord Jesus now brings these words of comfort that we read at verse 14:1, "let not your hearts be troubled." God's Son here in effect now says to His own, 'Yes, there is a lot happening to upset your hearts; however, in the midst of this turmoil, what each of you need to do is "believe in God (The Father), believe also in Me" (His Son). In other words, this is a time to trust, a time to put one's faith into practice!

As we see here, The Lord Jesus points the disciples to His Father, letting them know that they can trust Him, and at the same time they need to trust Him too, because He is God's Son among them. Since The Lord Jesus loves them and cares for them (noting again John 13:1), all that was being done for them here was for their good, even though they did not yet see this. The challenge for the disciples here, and for us too throughout our lives as children of God, is that faith has not yet become sight, and until it does, we are to trust God, to take Him at His word, and simply walk by faith!

Earlier at John 6:28,29, the crowds that were seeking for The Lord Jesus there asked Him, when they had finally found Him, "What shall we do, so that we may work the works of God?" To this question, God's Son had replied, "This is the work of God, that You believe in Him Whom He has sent." How much truer is this for those who have come to personally know God in salvation! May we honor and glorify God our precious Father by continually trusting in Him and in His precious Son, Whom He has graciously given for us. Let us also note what God further tells us at Romans 8:32, "He who did not spare His own Son, but delivered Him over for us all, how will He not also with Him freely give us all things?" Amen! All praise be to God for His love, mercy, and grace!

Then, after having encouraged the disciples to trust in God their Father, The Lord Jesus goes on to give them two promises to hold on to, as we now see at John 14:2,3, "[2] In My Father's house are many dwelling places; if it were not so, I would have told you; for I go to prepare a place for you. [3] If I go and prepare a place for you, I will come again and receive you to Myself, that where I am, there you may be also."

The first promise that God's Son gives these disciples and all His own here is, "...I go to prepare a place for you." One question we can ask here is: Where is that place? As The Lord Jesus points out here, it is "in My Father's House," which is Heaven (noting John 13:1,3; Acts 1:11; 1 Corinthians 15:47). We are also to note here that this place God's Son would then be in the process of preparing in Heaven would only be for those who have come to believe in Him at some point during their earthly life. In short, it is only for believers!

One question we would be warranted in also asking here is: What is it exactly that God's Son was returning to Heaven to prepare, which will be for believers in the future? The answer here is that after God's Son returned to Heaven, which would be after His ascension, He is there preparing a place for each believers in THE CITY that God has already prepared in Heaven (noting Hebrews 11:8-10,16).

This is the city we see coming down from Heaven to earth at Revelation 21:10, which city will be there during the 1000-year reign of God's Son over the nations of the earth during the fourth age of time. It will from this city that God's Son, The Lord Jesus Christ, will be ruling the earth from, doing so with all the believers of the first three ages of time, who will have undergone the first resurrection by then and will therefore now be in their new spiritual and now glorified bodies!

Then the second promise that God's Son gives the disciples here is as we see at verse 14:3, "If I go and prepare a place for you, I will come again and receive you to Myself, that where I am, there you may be also." As The Lord Jesus says here, if He goes to prepare a place for believers in Heaven, then it follows that He also has to return for believers, so that as believers we can all be with Him where He is. May it grip our hearts and minds here to realize as believers that when this occurs, we will ever be with our precious Lord Jesus! Then all believers will see Him (1 John 3:2), not just a few, and we will spend the fourth age serving Him and all eternity to come, never to be separated! All praise be to God in the Highest! Amen!

A further question we are free to ask here is: When will this occur? That is, when will The Lord Jesus return for us, who are the believers of this third age of time? In the context of the disciples that God's Son was physically Present with and speaking to here, since these were shortly to be part of the present third age at the coming of The Holy Spirit to indwell them, noting Acts 2:1-4 – namely in about fifty days from when this was spoken – then that return will be when The Holy Spirit is removed from the earth to end the present third age, as we see at 2 Thessalonians 2:6,7, with The Lord Jesus simultaneously coming to the just above to earth, as we see at 1 Thessalonians 4:14-17!

However, what we are to also grasp here is that even though God's Son has these disciples immediately in mind, we know that the truth being shared in this second promise here is true for every believer of the four ages of time. After The Lord Jesus' own resurrection from the dead, all those of the first age of time who had died from the time of Adam to just before Abraham were also raised and ascended with Him back to Heaven, as their part in the first resurrection, as we see at Matthew 27:52,53 and Ephesians 4:8-10.

Then immediately following the end of the present third age, God resumes and completes his program with the nation of Israel, during the seven years remaining to run its course of the second age of time. This second age will then end with the coming to earth again of The Lord Jesus Christ, now to establish His Kingdom for one thousand years. It is also at that second stage of His second coming that the believers of the second age of time will experience their part in the first resurrection, in that they will all be raised from the dead in turn to be with The Lord Jesus, noting Revelation 20:4-6.

What this means then is that the second promise in its full application relates to all those who are privileged to have a part in the first resurrection in time, which is all the believers of the four ages of time! For all of these, God's Son will have prepared a place in the city that God has prepared in Heaven and will come in time for them as part of the His first resurrection program, which relates only to the resurrection of all believers of time!

CHAPTER FIVE

A detailed look at the fourth PRIMARY texts of God's word relating the rapture of the church

What we will do in this chapter is to take a look at the fourth PRIMARY text of God's word relating to the rapture of the church, which is what God tells us at 2 Thessalonians 2:1, where we read, *"Now we request you, brethren, with regard TO THE COMING OF OUR LORD JESUS CHRIST AND OUR GATHERING TOGETHER TO HIM..."*

When the apostle Paul was led of God to say to the believers at Thessalonica here at 2 Thessalonians 2:1, "with regard to the coming of our Lord Jesus Christ and our gathering together to Him," he is making reference to the time the believers of the present third age of time will experience their part in the first resurrection, which will be at the first stage of The Lord Jesus Christ's second coming.

At 1 Thessalonians 4:14-17, we dealt with this event in detail, there seeing that ALL the believers of the present third age, bar none, will indeed be gathered to The Lord Jesus Christ in the clouds just above the earth, where each one will at that time experience glorification, where one's sinful nature will be removed from the soul, while one's body will simultaneously be changed into a spiritual body to last forever in God's Presence in Heaven!

CHAPTER SIX

A detailed look at the fifth PRIMARY texts of God's word relating the rapture of the church

What we will do in this chapter is to take a look at the fifth PRIMARY text of God's word relating to the rapture of the church, which is what God tells us at 2 Thessalonians 2:6,7, where we read, adding verses 3 and 4 for context, *"[3] Let no one in any way deceive you, for it will not come unless the apostasy comes first, and the man of lawlessness is revealed, the son of destruction,[4] who opposes and exalts himself above every so-called god or object of worship, so that he takes his seat in the temple of God, displaying himself as being God... [6] And you know what restrains him now, so that in his time he will be revealed. [7] For the mystery of lawlessness is already at work; only HE WHO NOW RESTRAINS WILL DO SO UNTIL HE IS TAKEN OUT OF THE WAY."*

And so, at 2 Thessalonians 2:6,7 here we are to note that there is One Who is now restraining the antichrist from coming upon the earth, who is in view here at verses 3 and 4, although "the mystery of lawlessness" as preparation for his coming is already "at work" in the world at present, even before this third age ends! And as we see here at verses 2:6,7, there is One in the world Who now restrains the operation of evil during the present third age.

The word "restrains" at both 2 Thessalonians 2:6,7 means 'to hold fast, hold back.' And the obvious question which arises here is: Who is The One in view here, Who is presently restraining evil in the world during the present third age, Who is then going to be "taken out of the way"?

There are five things that must be realized in answering this question here, with the first being that this is a PERSON Who is here in view, as restraining evil, since we read here, "HE who now restrains will do so until HE is taken out of the way." And secondly, we are to be aware that it is THE END OF THE PRESENT THIRD AGE, which is here in view at the same time as this Person doing the restraining is seen as being taken out of the way, which then results in evil being unleashed on earth with the coming of the antichrist on the world scene, as political leader over a one world government.

Then thirdly, we note the Person in view here as doing the restraining of the evil during the present third age does NOT remove Himself from the earth, but SOMEONE ELSE removes Him here at the end of the present third age. And fourthly, what should be clear to anyone looking at this and meditating upon it is that ONLY GOD HAS THE POWER TO RESTRAIN EVIL IN THE WORLD, as there is no human being that can ever possibly do so on the worldwide scale as we have in view here!

Then a fifth thing that also needs to be remembered here is that the present third age of time, also known as 'the church age,' started at Acts 2:1-4 WITH THE COMING TO EARTH OF THE HOLY SPIRIT, as given by God The Father through His Son, TO INDWELL THE HUMAN SPIRIT OF INDIVIDUAL BELIEVERS ON EARTH, TO FORM THE ONE BODY OF CHRIST ON EARTH, WHICH GOD REGARDS AS THE CHURCH!

In other words, this present third age STARTED with the coming of The Holy Spirit to indwell believers of earth, which together all form the one church of God. And so at the time the present third age ENDS, when we will be gathered to The precious Lord Jesus Christ, as we see at 1 Thessalonians 4:14-17 and 2 Thessalonians 2:1, which is at the time of our glorification, when believers of the present third age have their part in the first resurrection, and which takes place at the first stage of The Lord Jesus Christ's second coming at the end of the present age, THE HOLY SPIRIT IS THEN REMOVED FROM THE EARTH AS THE BODY OF CHRIST, namely all the believers of earth making up the church of God, ARE ALSO REMOVED FROM THE WHOLE OF THE EARTH and presented to our Lord Jesus Christ, Who is in the clouds, just above the earth, as we have seen at 1 Thessalonians 4:16,17! And so the answer to the question posed above is that it is The Holy Spirit, Who is the Restrainer at verses 6,7!

What then takes place simultaneously with The Holy Spirit gathering and bringing all believers of earth to The Lord Jesus Christ just above the earth is that the identity of the antichrist is revealed publicly on earth, and with this revealing, evil, which had before been restrained by the presence of The Holy Spirit indwelling believers throughout the earth, is no longer restrained, since The Holy Spirit and all believers of earth are now taken out of the way!

So what must be grasped and kept in mind here is that when we read at 2 Thessalonians 2:7 that "HE who now restrains will do so until HE is taken out of the way," we not only have The Holy Spirit being removed from the earth, but also all believers of earth making up the body of Christ on earth during the present third age also being removed AT THE VERY SAME TIME!

CHAPTER SEVEN

A detailed look at the sixth PRIMARY text of God's word relating the rapture of the church

What we will do in this chapter is to take a look at the sixth PRIMARY text of God's word relating to the rapture of the church, which is what God tells us at Romans 11:25, where we read, adding verse 26 for context, *"[25] For I do not want you, brethren, to be uninformed of this mystery — so that you will not be wise in your own estimation — that a partial hardening has happened to Israel UNTIL THE FULLNESS OF THE GENTILES HAS COME IN; [26] and so all Israel will be saved; just as it is written, "The Deliverer will come from Zion, He will remove ungodliness from Jacob.""*

When God speaks of "this mystery" here at verse 11:25, He is referring to spiritual truth which is outside the range of unassisted human apprehension, which can be known only as God makes it known by Divine revelation (as He is in the process of doing here at Romans 11:25, for instance), and only in a manner and at a time appointed by God, to those who are having truth illuminated to them by The Holy Spirit, due to having a personal relationship with God in salvation!

It is also important to keep in mind that God is still speaking to Gentile (that is, non-Jewish) believers here, as He makes "this mystery" known, and He says that the reason that He is disclosing this mystery at this time is "so that you (Gentiles) will not be wise in your own estimation," that is, that they will not start speculating within themselves about the future God has in store for the nation of Israel in His plan for the ages of time. And so, to avoid that occurring, God shares at verse 11:25 and into verse 11:26 a truth that He has never made known before, which is "that a partial hardening has happened to Israel until the fullness of the Gentiles has come in, and so all Israel will be saved…"

There are three truths in particular that are being given here by God at Romans 11:25 regarding the mystery that He is here in the process of disclosing, which we now need to explain in greater detail in order to understand what God is revealing to us here, which is to the Gentile believers of the present third age of time. The first truth to grasp here relates to what God means when He says, "a partial hardening has happened to Israel," which is the fact that the nation of Israel in this present third age – which is just one nation among the other nations of the earth – will remain in unbelief, that is, the majority of them will, as it is today in Israel, although there are some among them who are being saved!

This then leads to God's second truth that He is making known as part of "this mystery," which is that this state of affairs for the nation of Israel will continue "until the fullness of the Gentiles has come in;" which is now a reference to the fact that this present third age of time will not end until all the Gentile (non-Jewish) believers that God has appointed to eternal life in eternity past are saved in time!

When that last person to be saved in this present third age is saved, then there are two simultaneous events which occur at the same time, which is the removing of the believers of this present third age from the earth at the same time as God's Son returns to just above the earth, as we have seen at 1 Thessalonians 4:14-17, which is at the first stage of His second coming from Heaven to earth, which event occurs at the same time as God removes His Holy Spirit from the earth, as we have seen at 2 Thessalonians 2:6,7, as "He Who now restrains." Since The Holy Spirit indwells believers of the present third age, then His removal from the earth also means that believers are being removed at the same time, to meet God's Son in the clouds!

Then the third truth that God shares here, as part of "this mystery," is "and so all Israel will be saved," which now speaks of an event which takes place only after God's Son, The Lord Jesus Christ, has returned again from Heaven to this earth, as we see at Revelation 19:11-21, which is at the second stage of His second coming, in order to deal with the forces of the antichrist and the false prophet, who will have ruled on earth as one world political leader and one world religious leader under Satan, the devil, during the seven years remaining to run its course of the second age of time, in which God will have resumed His dealings with the nations of the earth through the believers of the nation of Israel.

And so, as to the meaning of the statement, "all Israel will be saved," we are to grasp that this is after God's Son has dealt with ALL unbelievers at the time of His return to earth at the end of those seven years, which means that ALL unbelievers from all nations on earth will die physically, which of course includes in all Gentile nations and also the nation of Israel, which is in accordance with what God makes known at Hebrew 9:27, where we read, "And inasmuch as it is appointed for men (that is, all unbelievers of earth) to die once and after this comes (God's) judgment...," in reference to His judgment of Revelation 20:11-15.

What this means then is that after God's Son has returned to earth and has dealt with the antichrist and the false prophet – which are the first and second beasts of Revelation 13:1 and 13:11 respectively – which will be as we read at Revelation 19:20, "And the beast (antichrist) was seized, and with him the false prophet (the second beast of Revelation 13;1) who performed the signs in his presence, by which he deceived those who had received the mark of the beast and those who worshiped his image; these two were thrown alive into the lake of fire which burns with brimstone."

Then when this has taken place, what we read at Matthew 24:31 will occur, where we read, "And He (God's Son) will send forth His angels with a great trumpet and they will gather together His elect (of the nation of Israel, who will not have died because elect of God unto salvation and therefore preserved by God until this moment, when their time of salvation has come) from the four winds, from one end of the sky to the other."

So what we are to see here is that when God says "all Israel will be saved," He is speaking of those of the nation of Israel who are elect of God from eternity past for salvation in time, with that time of salvation now having occurred, after the second stage of the second coming of God's Son from Heaven to earth! And since all the unbelievers of the nation of Israel will have died during that seven years left of the second age of time, then the "all Israel" needs to be seen as referring only to those that remain of the nation of Israel at that time, which will be the elect of God from eternity past!

That is why God goes on to say at the end of verse 11:26 here, "just as it is written (at Isaiah 59:20), "The Deliverer will come from Zion, He will remove ungodliness from Jacob." The "Deliverer" in view here is God's Son, having come from "Zion," which is "the holy city, Jerusalem," which will have come "down out of heaven from God," as we see at Revelation 21:10, which occurs as God's Son returns to earth from Heaven, as we see at Revelation 19:11, which is at the end of the seven years remaining of the second age of time. When all these events have taken place as part of "this mystery," then the fourth age of time will begin, which will last for 1000 years (noting Revelation 20:2,3,6), during which time God's Son will be ruling over the earth as King from that "holy city, Jerusalem," that has "come down out of heaven from God."

CHAPTER EIGHT

A detailed look at the seventh PRIMARY texts of God's word relating the rapture of the church

What we will do in this chapter is to take a look at the seventh PRIMARY text of God's word relating to the rapture of the church, which is what God tells us at Revelation 4:1,2, where we read, "[1] After these things I looked, and behold, A DOOR STANDING OPEN IN HEAVEN, and the first voice which I had heard, like the sound of a trumpet speaking with me, said, "COME UP HERE, and I will show you what must take place after these things." [2] IMMEDIATELY I WAS IN THE SPIRIT; AND BEHOLD, A THRONE WAS STANDING IN HEAVEN, and One sitting on the throne."

The words "After these things," repeated twice at verse 4:1 here, are indicative of a transition taking place, not only of a different age being in view, that is, from the third age back to complete the last seven years remaining of the second age of time; but is also indicative of A TRANSITION FROM EARTH TO HEAVEN! In other words, up to now, the apostle John has been on earth for what he has been enabled of God to see and for him to write down as the book of Revelation. But now, he will be for a time be describing events FROM THE PERSPECTIVE OF HEAVEN, where God dwells in His uncreated and eternal abode.

So the apostle John continues and says here, "I looked...," for we must remember that at Revelation 1:2, we are told that he had been chosen of God to write down for mankind "all that he saw." So we see God continue to show John what it is that he was to write down as the book of Revelation, which would have been around 90 AD. And he says, "behold," because this was something very important that God wanted us to be aware of, for what John now saw was "a door standing open in heaven..."

Since an open door is an invitation to walk through it, then it is not surprising for him to tell us what comes next, "and the first voice which I heard,, like the sound of a trumpet speaking with me," which is a reference back to Revelation 1:10, where God's Son, The Lord Jesus Christ, first spoke to the apostle John. At that time, as we see from Revelation 1:11, God's Son told John to write down all that he then saw concerning the seven local churches of Revelation 2 and 3. But now, God's Son speaks again to the apostle John and says, "COME UP HERE, and I will show you what must take place after these things." When we read here, "what must take place after these things," this is referring to what is contained in the rest of the book of Revelation, from Revelation Chapter 4 to 22, which is after the present third age of time!

And in saying, "Come up here...," it is obvious that the apostle John is here in the process of being given A VISION of seeing himself going up from where he was, which was on the earth, to Heaven, where God's Son was, at the right Hand of the throne of His Father, as we have seen at Revelation 3:21. However, God does not leave us guessing as to where this "here" was when John is then led to add at Revelation 4:2, "Immediately I was in the Spirit; and behold, a throne was standing open in heaven, and One sitting on the throne."

What God makes us aware of here is not only 'where' the apostle John was going to, which was Heaven, as God's uncreated and eternal abode; but also 'how' that was being made possible, which was, "Immediately I was in the Spirit..." It is important for us to realize here that John never went to Heaven bodily at this point, since this was still around 90 AD and not the time of glorification for the believers of the present third age, but rather in spirit only by the enablement of The Holy Spirit.

For what needs to be remembered is that it is impossible for a human being to enter Heaven bodily, before undergoing a transformation from the earthly to the spiritual, since Heaven is a spiritual place, noting 1 Corinthians 15:42-50. And we further need to remember that while a person is still alive physically, one still has a sinful nature, which is part of the soul; and no soul with a sinful nature can ever enter Heaven!

So that is why the apostle John was here supernaturally enabled of God to enter God's Presence in Heaven, which was only by his human spirit by the enablement of The Holy Spirit. In other words, when John says here, "Immediately I was in the Spirit," he is indicating what took place before he could even blink an eye, which was for him to be on earth one moment in time and then in the next to see himself in Heaven in spirit, which was instantaneously made possible by God The Father bringing it about through His Son by The Holy Spirit, which is always God's way of working.

So what is very important for us to grasp here is that the apostle John is being given a picture of what will take place at the end of the third age of time, when the glorification of all the believers of the present third age takes place; that is, when all these believers will be brought to Heaven in their new resurrection bodies, as we see at 1 Thessalonians 4:14-17.

Then we note that the apostle John is led of God to exclaim once more – for we need to remember that all of this is God's word, with John only being led of God to write it down by the enablement of The Holy Spirit, noting 2 Peter 1:20,21 – "behold," that is, 'pay attention, this is important,' for what John sees first as he sees himself in Heaven in spirit by The Holy Spirit is "a throne standing in heaven, and One sitting on the throne." And here we need to note that the word "standing" which would have been better translated as 'set;' so that what John saw was a throne set in Heaven.

Then the word "sitting" is in reference to the position of The Person on the throne, which is here to be seen as God The Father, which we know for sure based on what we are told in the rest of the chapter, in that it is to Him that all worship is here directed. That it is God The Father on the throne here is also clear from comparing this chapter with Revelation 5:1-7, and also Revelation 1:4,8 with Revelation 4:8.

Then the word "throne," repeated twice here at Revelation 4:2 , refers to God's seat of authority. What needs to ever be remembered here then is that this is Heaven, where everything is spiritual and not physical. What this means is that while the throne is real, in that it does exist, nevertheless, it is not something physical, which can be touched tangibly, as we would touch the throne of one of royalty here on earth.

Before going further, we should give careful thought to what we have just been told at Revelation 4:1,2 here, especially keeping in mind that what is about to begin at Revelation 6 is a resumption of the second age of time, in order to complete the last seven years of it. And since at Revelation 2 and 3 we had the length of the present third age in view, this therefore means that the believers of the third age would have experienced their part in the first resurrection relating to believers, which further means that now their time of glorification would have occurred. So when we have the apostle John, who was part of this third age, being brought to Heaven in spirit in His day, then it is to be seen as a picture of God removing His church from the earth, which is all the believers of the present third age, and bringing them all to Heaven at the end of it, because their time of glorification has come! This is again the event which God has had in view at 1 Thessalonians 4:14-17.

What is being pointed out here then is that since the end of Revelation 3 is the end of the present third age, and since beginning at Revelation 6:1 pictures the resumption again of the second age of time in order to complete it, with seven years left to run its course, then this means that we have Revelation 4 and 5 in between these two events. And the question facing us is: What is God intending for us to see from these two chapters?

God already gave us a clue to that question from what we have seen at Revelation 4:1,2 already, which is the apostle John being brought to Heaven in spirit by The Holy Spirit, which is a picture of God's church on earth, as all the believers of the third age of time, being brought to Heaven by The Holy Spirit, due to the fact that now their part in the first resurrection has come, namely their time of glorification, when God removes the sinful nature from the soul and gives each a new spiritual body to now enter His Presence in Heaven!

What this means then is that Revelation 4 and 5 here are intended by God to be a picture of God's church in Heaven, which is all the believers of earth of the third age of time being there now in glorified bodies, and seeing what happens from there regarding the events of the last seven years of the second age of time, which would be taking place on earth, beginning at Revelation 6! In other words, Revelation 4 and 5 is what takes place in Heaven while Revelation 6 to 19:21 takes place on earth during the exact same seven year period left of the second age of time!

CHAPTER NINE

A detailed look at the first to the sixth secondary texts of God's word relating to the rapture of the church

What we will do in this chapter is take a look at all six SECONDARY texts of God's word relating to the rapture of the church, doing so in one chapter here for two reasons. One is that these texts, while important, are not as important and comprehensive as the PRIMARY texts that we have looked at from Chapter Two to Chapter Eight. And the second reason is that what can be said about these texts will be fairly brief, at least for the most part.

The first SECONDARY text of God's word relating to the rapture of the church

The first SECONDARY text, where the rapture is partially also in view, is at Ephesians 5:27, where we read, adding verses 25 and 26 for context, *"[25] Husbands, love your wives, just as Christ also loved the church and gave Himself up for her, [26] so that He might sanctify her, having cleansed her by the washing of water with the word, [27] THAT HE MIGHT PRESENT TO HIMSELF THE CHURCH IN ALL HER GLORY, HAVING NO SPOT OR WRINKLE OR ANY SUCH THING; BUT THAT SHE WOULD BE HOLY AND BLAMELESS."*

As we see from verse 5:25 here, God appeals to believing husbands to do in the realm of the physical, which is to "love your wives," which He bases on what is already true in the realm of the spiritual, as we see from verses 5:25-27, "just as Christ also loved the church (having in view here all the believers of the present third age of time) and gave Himself up for her (speaking here of His death at the cross, where He removed the sin barrier in Himself between a sinful human race and God), so that He might sanctify her (that is, that all believers comprising His church on earth might be set apart for God's will after one's salvation), having cleansed her by the washing of water with the word (here God using the imagery of the physical to illustrate what took place at salvation, where God, by His Holy Spirit, took His word containing the gospel, and brought us to faith in Himself through that word, which had His precious Son as its focus, thereby washing us of all our sins, noting Titus 3:5 and 1 Peter 1:23), that He might present to Himself the church in all her glory (that is, all believers at the time of the end of the present third age of time, as we have seen already at 1 Thessalonians 4:14-17)), having no spot or wrinkle or any such thing; but that she would be holy and blameless" (because now in God's Presence in a glorified state, that is, with the sinful nature removed from the soul and one's physical body transformed to a spiritual body to last forever, noting 1 Corinthians 15:42-44 with Philippians 3:20,21)!

The second SECONDARY text of God's word relating to the rapture of the church

Then a second SECONDARY text that we need to note here is at Philippians 3:20,21, where we read, *"[20] For our citizenship is in heaven, from which also WE EAGERLY WAIT FOR A SAVIOR, THE LORD JESUS CHRIST; [21] WHO WILL TRANSFORM THE BODY OF OUR HUMBLE STATE INTO CONFORMITY WITH THE BODY OF HIS GLORY, BY THE EXERTION OF THE POWER THAT HE HAS even to subject all things to Himself."*

As God makes clear at Philippians 3:20,21 above that this earth is not the home of believers, which therefore means we are not to live for this life on earth only, but be mindful of our more permanent place, as where we will all eventually be as believers; for as we further see here, our citizenship as believers is in Heaven, as God's eternal and uncreated dwelling place, which we are all destined for!

And so, all going to our real home is something that all believers are looking for, as we all wait for God's precious Son, The Lord Jesus Christ, to come, which will mean the time of our glorification has come, as we have seen at 1 Thessalonians 4:14-17 already, when all believers of the present third age of time are all conformed to His image, in that He "will transform the body of our humble state into conformity with the body of His glory, by the exertion of the power that He has even to subject all things to Himself."

In other words, we will have at that moment our sinful nature removed from the soul once and for all, as the source of our lifelong sinful acts; and we will all have our bodies changed from physical bodies to spiritual ones to last forever (noting 1 Corinthians 15:42-44), since God's dwelling place, where we are all going, is a spiritual place, where God is a spirit Being (noting John 4:24), and all the angelic beings there are spiritual also!

The third SECONDARY text of God's word relating to the rapture of the church

A third SECONDARY text of God's word, where the rapture is again partially in view, is at 1 Thessalonians 1:10, adding verse 9 for context, *"[9] For they themselves report about us what kind of a reception we had with you, and how you turned to God from idols to serve a living and true God, [10] AND TO WAIT FOR HIS SON FROM HEAVEN, whom He raised from the dead, THAT IS JESUS, WHO RESCUES US FROM THE WRATH TO COME."*

As we then see from 1 Thessalonians 1:9,10 here, the apostle Paul was led of God to state three things which were being reported from believers elsewhere, who had contact with the believers from Thessalonica, namely: 1) "what kind of a reception we had with you," then 2) "how you turned to

73

God from idols to serve a living and true God," and 3) "and to wait for His Son from heaven."

Since the first two things just mentioned do not concern us here for the purpose of this book, we will only look at the third thing mentioned here, which is at verse 10. And so, the word "wait" at verse 10 has the thought of 'waiting with patience and confident expectancy." And so, when we are told here at 1 Thessalonians 1:10 regarding the believers at Thessalonica, "and to wait for His Son from heaven, whom He raised from the dead, that is Jesus, who rescues us from the wrath to come," we are to observe from this that these believers had obviously been taught by the apostle Paul and his companions in ministry about The precious Lord Jesus Christ's second coming from Heaven to earth, and particularly the first stage of that return relating to believers of the present third age, also known as the church!

In other words, what is in view here is what we have seen already at 1 Thessalonians 4:14-17, namely that God The precious Father will be sending His precious Son, The Lord Jesus Christ, to just above the earth to receive to Himself all believers comprising the body of Christ on earth, the church, which is at the first stage of The Lord Jesus Christ's second coming from Heaven to earth. The second stage of that second coming does not take place until approximately seven years later.

It is clear from the statement, "to wait for His Son from Heaven," that God's Son, The Lord Jesus Christ, is already in Heaven, as God's eternal and uncreated abode, and that He is coming again to earth, which is a truth that The Lord Jesus Himself shared with His disciples the night He was betrayed, as we have seen already from John 14:1-3, which we note again here for our present purpose, "[1] Do not let your heart be troubled; believe in God (The Father), believe also in Me (The Son). [2] In My Father's house are many dwelling places; if it were not so, I would have told you; for I go to prepare a place for you. [3] If I go and prepare a place for you, I will come again and receive you to Myself, that where I am, there you may be also." It is that promised coming and being received by Him and being where The Son of God presently is that believers of the present third age are waiting for!

It is important to note that God The Father Himself identifies "Jesus" as being "His Son" at verse 1:10 here, Who is also identified as being The One Whom God The Father "raised from the dead," which is amply testified to by God in His word, noting for instance what God tells us at Acts 2:22-24, "[22] Men of Israel, listen to these words: Jesus the Nazarene, a man attested to you by God with miracles and wonders and signs which God performed through Him in your midst, just as you yourselves know - [23] this Man, delivered over by the predetermined plan and foreknowledge of God, you nailed to a cross by the hands of godless men and put Him to death. [24] But God raised Him up again, putting an end to the agony of death, since it was impossible for Him to be held in its power." God wants all to know and believe that this "Jesus" was no ordinary human being, but rather, He is The Son of God in human flesh, now glorified (that is, now raised from the dead and ascended to glory, noting Acts 1:9-11 with Hebrews 1:2,3)!

Then the further statement at 1 Thessalonians 1:10, "who rescues us from the wrath to come," needs to be seen in the context of believers being promised by God that they will not be experiencing "the wrath to come" by virtue of having believed in God through faith in His precious Son, The Lord Jesus Christ, Who has borne the wrath of God for the whole human race when He hung on the cross of Calvary during those three hours of darkness, which came from twelve noon to three in the afternoon, noting for instance what God tells us at Mark 15:33, "When the sixth hour came (which is 12 noon, counting from sunup at 6 am), darkness fell over the whole land until the ninth hour" (3 pm).

The word "rescues" here at verse 1:10 speaks of 'to rescue from, to preserve from, and so, to deliver.' And as was already mentioned, believers of the present third age will be kept, preserved, delivered by God The precious Father through His precious Son by The precious Holy Spirit from

75

experiencing "the wrath to come," which in the present context does NOT refer to the time of wrath coming on all unbelievers of time after the final judgment of time, which results in all unbelievers of time, along with all fallen angels, being cast by God away from His Presence forever in the lake of fire, which is eternal hell.

In one having come to know God in salvation means one will never have to experience that final wrath of God in time; however, "the wrath to come" here at verse 1:10 must be seen as referring to a time of wrath that is coming in the seven years remaining of the second age of time, but which cannot begin until the present third age ends with all the believers of the present age have been removed from the earth, since God never judges the unbelievers of this world with the believers still present in their midst, having given evidence of this in human history already at the time of judgment in the worldwide flood, and also at the time of His judgment of Sodom and Gomorrah, when Noah and Lot, and their families, were removed from the scene of judgment when God did bring judgment on unbelievers on earth in their day!

Therefore, the "wrath to come" here is to be seen as what begins on earth at the Hand of God the moment that believers of the present third age have been removed from the scene of earth. And how do we know this to be true? Simply because there are no other comings from Heaven to earth of God's Son, The Lord Jesus Christ, but that seen as the first stage of it at the end of this third age, which God tells us about at 1 Thessalonians 4:14-17, and that second stage of that second coming at the end of the last seven years of God's second age, when God's Son will be dealing with the unbelievers of the nations of the earth, as God tells us at Revelation 19:11-21.

And so, the "wrath to come" which God has in view at verse 1:10 is that time of judgment on all unbelievers of the world during the seven years of the second age of time to follow the present third age. We should be aware here that this time of "wrath to come" is spoken of by God in many passages of the

Old Testament, for instance at Isaiah 63:6; Jeremiah 30:7; Zephaniah 1:14,15,18; and also in the New Testament, noting for instance at Revelation 6:1 to Revelation 19:21.

It is important to keep in mind that the second stage of the second coming of God's Son from Heaven to earth, which occurs approximately seven years after the first stage of His second coming, based on the prophecy of Daniel 9:24-27, is not in view at all here at 1 Thessalonians 1:10.

The fourth SECONDARY text of God's word relating to the rapture of the church

A fourth SECONDARY text where the rapture of the church is again partially in view is at 1 Thessalonians 2:19, where we read, adding verse 20 for context, *"[19] For who is our hope or joy or crown of exultation? Is it not even you, IN THE PRESENCE OF OUR LORD JESUS AT HIS COMING? [20] For you are our glory and joy."*

We note from 1 Thessalonians 2:19,20 here that when the apostle Paul one day stands in the Presence of The Lord Jesus Christ "at His coming" – having in view here the first stage of His second coming, as especially seen at 1 Thessalonians 4:14-17, which is part of the first resurrection relating to believers – at that time believers like the Thessalonians, and not them alone, will be his "glory and joy," "hope," and "crown of exultation," in the sense that they will have proved to be true children of God, who had come to know God, as a work of God's grace and power, through his ministry of the preaching of the gospel.

The word "crown" here at 1 Thessalonians 2:19 is in reference to 'that which surrounds, or encircles,' which is here seen to be an emblem of future life, joy, reward, and glory in the Presence of God's Son at the first stage of His second coming for all the believers of the present third age, with the Thessalonian believers being a small part of that total group. Therefore, the "crown" in view here is not literal, which is further confirmed in that believers themselves are that crown, also noting what we read at Philippians 4:1, "Therefore, my beloved brethren whom I long to see, my joy and crown (same word), in this way stand firm in the Lord, my beloved."

The word "exultation" here relates to the fact that the Thessalonians, as is also true of all other believers elsewhere who came to know God through the apostle Paul's ministry, will be the basis for his boast in The Lord, not in the sense of sinful pride, but rather in the sense of glorying in what God has done through him for His own eternal glory and praise!

Then the word "hope" also here at 1 Thessalonians 2:19 speaks of a 'favorable and confident expectation' relating to the future, which as already mentioned, relates here to the time of their part in the first resurrection of believers of the present third age, at the first stage of the second coming of God's Son from Heaven to earth, The Lord Jesus Christ. Since the Thessalonians were a genuine work of God's grace and power, then this was further evidence for the apostle Paul himself of a favorable and confident expectation of the life that is coming beyond the grave!

The fifth SECONDARY text of God's word relating to the rapture of the church

Then a fifth SECONDARY text of God's word, where the rapture is also partially in view, is at 1 Thessalonians 3:13, adding verses 11 and 12 for context, *"[11] Now may our God and Father Himself and Jesus our Lord direct our way to you; [12] and may the Lord cause you to increase and abound in love for one another, and for all people, just as we also do for you; [13] so that He may establish your hearts without blame in holiness before our God and Father AT THE COMING OF OUR LORD JESUS WITH ALL HIS SAINTS."*

As we see from 1 Thessalonians 3:11-13 here, the apostle Paul is led of God to pray that God The Father, working through His Son, which is always by The Holy Spirit, might open the way for him to go to them, but until He does, Paul's prayer is threefold, namely that: 1) "the Lord cause you to increase;" 2) "and abound in love for one another, and for all people, just as we also do for you," and 3) "so that He may establish your hearts without blame in holiness before our

God and Father at the coming of our Lord Jesus with all His saints."

And again, since only the third part of the prayer, which is verse 3:13 as what concerns us in this book, this is therefore what we will concentrate on here. And so, we note that the apostle Paul prays here that the hearts of the believers at Thessalonica might be without blame in holiness, that is, without known unconfessed sins in their lives, being able to stand before God unashamed when The Lord Jesus Christ returns again for them at the end of the present third age, this being at the first stage of His second coming, which we have already had in view at 1 Thessalonians 1:10; 2:19, and also at 4:14-17, which here at 1 Thessalonians 3:13 is described as "at the coming of our Lord Jesus with all His saints."

What is also important to note here is that the expression "with all His saints," refers to those believers making up God's church on earth during the present third age, who would have died physically and whose human spirit would already be in Heaven, and whose spirit is now returning to earth with The Lord Jesus Christ, because their part in the first resurrection, relating to believers of the present third age, would now have arrived, due to the first stage of The Lord Jesus' second coming from Heaven to earth having now come.

The sixth SECONDARY text of God's word relating to the rapture of the church

And then a sixth SECONDARY text of God's word where the same event is also in view is at 1 John 3:2,3, where God says to us, *"[2] Beloved, now we are children of God, and it has not appeared as yet what we will be. We know that WHEN HE APPEARS, WE WILL BE LIKE HIM, BECAUSE WE WILL SEE HIM JUST AS HE IS. [3] AND EVERYONE WHO HAS THIS HOPE fixed on Him purifies himself, just as He is pure."*

When God says at 1 John 3:2 above, "Beloved, now we are children of God, and it has not appeared as yet what we will be. We know that when He appears, we will be like Him, because we will see Him just as He is," He there says two things we know for sure. One is that we are children of God, and two is that when God's Son, The Lord Jesus Christ, appears again at the end of this present third age, which is the time of glorification for believers of this present third age, then we will all be changed into the image of God's Son in an instant, with our sinful nature removed from us and our bodies changed into spiritual bodies so that they will now last forever in Heaven, where we will be forever with God.

This will be so for us as believers simply because this was so for God's Son, Who is a Pattern for not only our present life now on earth, but also for all eternity in Heaven. Let us note what God tells us in this regard at Romans 8:29,30, "[29] For those whom He foreknew, HE ALSO PREDESTINED TO BECOME CONFORMED TO THE IMAGE OF HIS SON, SO THAT HE WOULD BE THE FIRSTBORN AMONG MANY BRETHREN; [30] and these whom He predestined, He also called; and these whom He called, He also justified; and these whom He justified, He also glorified."

Here God sees believers from eternity past until each is in Heaven with Him at glorification, even though this has not yet taken place for all believers of time; only for those of the first age. And so, before time began, God knew us as His own because that is when He first chose us for Himself out of all human beings freely rejecting Him, and it was then that He predestined us to become His through salvation in time. Then when time began with His original creation of all things, including angelic beings and human beings, God called and justified (that is, brought salvation to) all those whom He had foreknown and predestined in eternity past. And then the believers of each of the four ages of time are brought to Heaven through glorification each at their proper time and order, as we see from 1 Corinthians 15:22,23.

Coming back to 1 John 3:2, we then see that the only thing we do not know is "what we will be." What God is making reference to here is our new spiritual bodies, which we will have in glorification. We do know that these bodies will be like that of God's Son, The Lord Jesus Christ, now glorified, which is a spiritual body, as we have seen from what God tells us at 1 Corinthians 15:42-44,49. However, since God has never given us a picture of what His precious Son looks like, which is why He forbids making any graven image of Him (Exodus 20:4), then that is also true of us, in that we will not know what we will look like until that time of glorification occurs. God is saying here that He will not disclose that to us until then. All we know at present is that we will have a spiritual body in resurrection, because God's Son now has one, and we will be like Him in terms of now sinless forever due to our sinful nature having now been removed from us. But that is the extent of what God has presently revealed to us!

One thing that I personally believe here is that we will all be around 33 years of age in glorification, since that is the age God's Son was at when He was glorified after His being raised from the dead the third day. And this is likely the age that Adam and Eve were at when first created by God, because thirty-three years of age refers to one who is fully grown in every way, physically, emotionally, and mentally.

What this also means then is that there are no babies, young children, or seniors in Heaven, but we will all be like the angels (Luke 20:34-36), neither male nor female, having only what is required in order to exist in that spiritual realm. For instance, we will no longer have a stomach and elimination system, as there will be nothing physical of nature there (noting 1 Corinthians 6:13). God is a spirit Being (John 4:24), the angels are spirit beings, and Heaven is a spiritual place, which means that we too will therefore become spiritual beings fitted for that very real place forever!

And now based on all God has prepared for believers for both time and eternity, this brings a responsibility, as God makes clear at 1 John 3:3, "And everyone who has this hope fixed on Him purifies himself, just as He is pure." When God speaks of "this hope fixed on Him" here, He is making reference to what awaits us past the grave. That is our hope, to experience all that His own precious Son experienced Himself as He went before us, noting what God says at 2 Corinthians 4:14, "knowing that He (God The Father) who raised the Lord Jesus will raise us also with Jesus (at the first stage of His second coming) and will present us with you."

Since the hope of every believer of time is life with God past the grave, then all believers of every age of time have the same responsibility toward God, which is that "everyone… purifies himself, just as He is pure." In other words, knowing that we will all one day soon have the same image as God's Son forever, Who is sinless, then we too need to start now in being pure, which is without known unconfessed sins in our lives, which is what "being pure" means here.

CHAPTER TEN

Dealing with possible questions that might arise relating to the coming rapture of the church!

As with any subject matter, there are always questions that tend to arise, especially from those encountering a subject matter for the first time, and especially when dealing with rapture of the church, which is not only a miraculous event, but is also a unique event to us, in that we have never experienced it before, which means that there is a mysterious element surrounding the subject. And so, in this chapter, we will attempt to deal with some possible questions that might arise from the coming rapture of the church, as God has made it known to us especially at 1 Thessalonians 4:14-17, that we have looked at in Chapter Two, and also at 1 Corinthians 15:35-50, which we have looked at in Chapter Three.

One possible question might be: What about those on earth who are inside a building, a car, a bus, a train, or a plane, when the rapture occurs?

What the question entails here is how does one go through a physical structure to go meet The Lord Jesus in the air above the earth at the time the rapture comes! As was pointed out in Chapter Two, and as we also saw in Chapter Three, we who are alive when that event occurs will immediately have our physical bodies changed into spiritual bodies, as we rise to meet The Lord Jesus in the air, which means that in now

83

having a spiritual body, we are able to go through any physical structure we might find ourselves in at the time!

What we need to remember here is that at the moment the rapture occurs, which is an instantaneous snatching of us from the earth by God to meet His Son in the clouds above the earth, we will be leaving behind everything that is of a physical nature, such as shoes, clothing, jewelry, cell phones, ear pieces, wigs, dentures, metal and plastic pins and plates that might be in our bodies, including pacemakers, etc! Only our body, which will now be spiritual in nature, will now be rising to meet God's Son in the air!

What would prove useful at this point would be to take an example from the life of God's precious Son while on earth at His first coming, as for instance noting what we see take place at John 20:19 and 20:26,27, which relates to The Lord Jesus Christ immediately after His resurrection from the dead, and so there reading, *"{19] So when it was evening on that day, the first day of the week, and when the doors were shut where the disciples were, for fear of the Jews, Jesus came and stood in their midst and said to them, "Peace be with you... [26] After eight days His disciples were again inside, and Thomas with them. Jesus came, the doors having been shut, and stood in their midst and said, "Peace be with you." [27] Then He said to Thomas, "Reach here with your finger, and see My hands; and reach here your hand and put it into My side; and do not be unbelieving, but believing.""*

What is important to grasp here is that The Lord Jesus now had A SPIRITUAL BODY in resurrection, one that could be SEEN AND TOUCHED, as is clear from verse 27! However, what is very important to see here, relating specifically to our question, is that at verse 19 and again at verse 26, God's Son SUDDENLY APPEARS IN THE MIDST OF THE DISCIPLES, with God making sure here that we have the information provided regarding both appearances, namely that THE DOORS WERE SHUT, so that we might realize that The Lord Jesus did not enter through the door here in order to be with His disciples!

What this means then, for our present purpose, is that just as God's Son could go through a physical door, due to now having a spiritual body in resurrection, so too will that be the case with us when our time comes on God's timetable for us to have our part in the first resurrection, we too will have a spiritual body to go through any physical structure we might find ourselves in at the time, to immediately then find ourselves in the Presence of God's Son in the clouds just above the earth!

Another possible question here could be: What if I am a pilot of a plane, or a bus driver, or a train conductor, or driving a transport truck, or a carload of people when the rapture occurs? Will that not likely cause the death of all those who are being transported at the time, if I, as a believer, am suddenly removed from the earth?

What is being asked here is more than likely going to happen when the rapture of the believers of the present third age occurs, who being still alive are suddenly removed from the earth! But let us keep in mind that all those in those vehicles mentioned here who are believers at that time will also be removed at the same time, and not just the person at the wheel. This may of course mean the death of those left behind if there is a plane crash, a bus crash, and so forth, at the time of the rapture; but these left behind will have been the unbelievers, who are in the process of experiencing the judgment of God for not having believed in His Son!

For what needs to be remembered here is that as this present third age ends with the removal of the believers from the earth, along with The Holy Spirit indwelling each of those believers being raptured, this means that "the day of The Lord" immediately starts, which means not only a time of judgment on all the unbelievers left on earth at this time, but this is also a resumption of the second age of time, in which God now completes the last seven years left of it!

What we are also to keep in mind here is that this means that the events of Revelation 6:1 to Revelation 19:21 now take place on earth, in which a third of the unbelievers of earth at present will die during that seven years of God's judgment (noting Revelation 9:15,18). And let us not forget that since God has removed His Holy Spirit from the earth, then that means that there is no restraint at all from evil taking place on earth during this time! God is stating something that is absolutely true when it is recorded of Him at Hebrews 10:31, "It is a terrifying thing to fall into the hands of the living God, " and also at Hebrews 12:29, "for our God is a consuming fire."

And so, the fact that many unbelievers will immediately die as a result of the believers of the present third age being removed from the earth should not surprise us, for this truly is a time of evil let loose, of great chaos and upheaval, of horrendous violence and death, simply because it is a time of God's judgment on the unbelievers left on earth!

CHAPTER ELEVEN

Even some Christian hymns speak to us of the coming rapture of the church!

As believers, we have most likely often noticed how so many Christian hymns end in the last stanza with a reference to the rapture of the church. Most of these hymns were intentionally originally written to put down on paper the truths of God's word, and then when musically arranged as hymns for singing by believers, one and all might be reminded of the truths one has read in God's word!

And so, in this chapter we will look at the last stanza of three such hymns as examples of this, although the reader might no doubt be able to come up with many more. So let us begin with the words of the last stanza of the hymn, "Hallelujah! What A Savior!," which reads as follows: "When He comes, our glorious King, All His ransomed home to bring, Then anew this song we'll sing: Hallelujah! What a Savior!"

The last stanza of a second hymn that we can note here is that of "The Solid Rock," which ends with the words, "When He shall come with trumpet sound, O may I then in Him be found: Dressed in His righteousness alone, Faultless to stand before the throne. On Christ, the solid Rock I stand: All other ground is sinking sand."

Then the last stanza of a third hymn we can further make note of here is "One Day, which ends with the words, "One

87

day the trumpet will sound for His coming, One day the skies with His glory will shine; Wonderful day, my beloved ones bringing! Glorious Savior, this Jesus is mine!"

As we can see in each of the above three hymns mentioned, there is some aspect of the truth of the rapture of the church in view here, as a reminder to believers of the present third age each time such hymns as these are sung that there is a glorious day coming, which could even be today!

CHAPTER TWELVE

Grasping the fact that 1 Corinthians 15:51-57 DOES NOT refer to the rapture of the church!

The purpose of this present chapter is to show that 1 Corinthians 15:51-57 DOES NOT REFER TO THE RAPTURE OF THE CHURCH, in that it does not refer to the believers of the present third age of time being brought to Heaven at the first stage of the second coming of God's Son from Heaven to earth, as we have seen disclosed by God at 1 Thessalonians 4:13-18 in Chapter Two and also at 1 Corinthians 15:35-50 in Chapter Three.

As will now be shown here, this passage actually refers to what occurs at the end of the fourth age of time, when the believers then alive, including those believers who have died, will likewise all be brought to Heaven by God as their part in the fourth stage of the first resurrection, including being told of the resurrection of all the unbelievers of the four ages of time, so that at that point in time God will have then removed physical death from His original creation!

As we go through these verses word by word, we will be seeing that these verses indeed do not refer to the rapture of the church, even though this a common teaching today, which is largely due to one not having a good grasp of God's resurrection program in time, namely the four stages of the first resurrection relating only to all the believers of time, and then to the one encompassing resurrection for all the unbelievers of time all at once as time comes to an end!

And so, to begin with here, let us note what God says at 1 Corinthians 15:51-57, where we read, *"[51] Behold, I tell you a mystery; we will not all sleep, but we will all be changed, [52] in a moment, in the twinkling of an eye, at the last trumpet; for the trumpet will sound, and the dead will be raised imperishable, and we will be changed. [53] For this perishable must put on the imperishable, and this mortal must put on immortality. [54] But when this perishable will have put on the imperishable, and this mortal will have put on immortality, then will come about the saying that is written, "Death is swallowed up in victory. [55] O death, where is your victory? O death, where is your sting?" [56] The sting of death is sin, and the power of sin is the law; [57] but thanks be to God, who gives us the victory through our Lord Jesus Christ."*

We note that at verse 51, the apostle Paul is led of God to say, "Behold," in other words, this is very important, so pay special attention to this. And then he goes on and says, " I tell you A MYSTERY," which we need to remember is referring to spiritual truth which is outside the range of unassisted human apprehension, which can be known only as God makes it known by Divine revelation (as He is in the process of doing here, for instance), and only in a manner and at a time appointed by God, to those who are having truth illuminated to them by The Holy Spirit, due to having a personal relationship with God in salvation!

And as God begins to disclose the "mystery" here, He says through the apostle Paul, "we will not all sleep, but we will all be changed...," which is NOT the mystery per se here, for God has already made this truth known at 1 Thessalonians 4:14-17 that not all believers of the present third age will die physically, as some will still be alive when God's Son returns from Heaven at the first stage of His second coming. However, as He shared there, all believers, whether dead or alive, will be changed from a physical body to a spiritual body, as what God has also already disclosed to us at 1 Corinthians 15:35-50!

WHAT IS part of the mystery here, however, is what God goes on to disclose from hereon in, as He next tells us at verse 52, that the change from the physical body to the spiritual body takes place, "in a moment, in the twinkling of an eye." In other words, that change from the physical to the spiritual occurs as fast as a person can close and open one's eyelids! So what we have just had disclosed to us here is a truth that had never been disclosed before.

Then the second part of the mystery that God shares here, also at verse 52, is that this change from the physical body to a spiritual body of those here in view takes place, "AT THE LAST TRUMPET." And the obvious question which comes to mind here is: What does God mean here by "the last trumpet"? A study of the word "trumpet" in God's word has shown that what is in view here, "at the last trumpet," is a reference to the time when the seventh trumpet will sound, of the seven trumpet judgments of God that He discloses as coming upon the unbelievers of this earth during the last seven years remaining of the second age of time, which will have resumed immediately as the present third age of time will have been completed with the rapture of the church!

And so, let us note Revelation 8:2,6 where God first makes known to mankind those seven trumpet judgments, there reading, "[2] And I saw the seven angels who stand before God, and seven trumpets were given to them.... [6] And the seven angels who had the seven trumpets prepared themselves to sound them." However, we are to note that the seventh trumpet, which is the "last trumpet" of 1 Corinthians 15:52 only occurs at Revelation 11:15.

And before we go to Revelation 11:15 and that seventh (and last) trumpet of time, we need to note what God says about that seventh (and last trumpet) of time at Revelation 10:7, where we read, "but in the days of the voice of the seventh angel, when he is about to sound, THEN THE MYSTERY OF GOD IS FINISHED, as He preached to His servants the prophets." In other words, the seventh trumpet and third woe, which we note here will not be seen until Revelation 11:15, actually takes us to the end of time, right up to the eternal state, so that by the time that seventh angel comes on the world scene all that God has prophesied of what will happen in time, and is contained in His word, will all have been completed as part of that seventh trumpet and third woe! Let us note, for instance, what God says at Amos 3:7, in regards to the last part of verse 10:7 here, "Surely the Lord God does nothing unless He reveals His secret counsel to His servants the prophets."

We are to note that the word "preached" at Revelation 10:7 means to declare, or bring, or announce glad tidings. In a study of this word in Scripture, it was concluded that the word "preached" at Revelation 10:7 referred to the good news that God made known to the prophets of the Old Testament, regarding what would take place in the future, and which always has His precious Son as the central focus!

We are to also to see from verse 10:7 here that the word "mystery" again denotes not the mysterious, as in the English word, but that which, being outside the range of unassisted natural apprehension, can be made known only by Divine revelation, and is made known in a manner and at a time appointed by God, and only to those who are illumined by His Holy Spirit. In the ordinary sense, a mystery implies knowledge withheld, but its Scriptural significance, it is truth revealed. Therefore, when God says here that "the mystery of God is finished," once the seventh trumpet and the third woe is reached, means that all the truth that God has given in time, which centers principally on His precious Son, Who is good news indeed, will all have been fulfilled by the time this last trumpet has sounded, which is what the word "finished" refers to here!

Then if we now turn to Revelation 11:15, we will now see that this is when the seventh angel sounds the seventh and "last trumpet" of time. So let us note Revelation 11:15-18 here and see what God there discloses to us, which we will be looking at in detail, because what we read here is God disclosing what does take place in time at that "last trumpet" that we are presently looking at in 1 Corinthians 15:52.

And so, at Revelation 11:15-18 we read, *"[15] Then the seventh angel sounded; and there were loud voices in heaven, saying, "The kingdom of the world has become the kingdom of our Lord and of His Christ; and He will reign forever and ever." [16] And the twenty-four elders, who sit on their thrones before God, fell on their faces and worshiped God, [17] saying, "We give You thanks, O Lord God, the Almighty, who are and who were, because You have taken Your great power and have begun to reign. [18] And the nations were enraged, and Your wrath came, and the time came for the dead to be judged, and the time to reward Your bond-servants the prophets and the saints and those who fear Your name, the small and the great, and to destroy those who destroy the earth."*

We are to note that the apostle John, who was chosen by God to write down the book of Revelation for us, is here being led of God to describe what he next sees at Revelation 11:15-18, which is a series of events taking place in Heaven, as God's eternal and uncreated abode. And here, at Revelation 11:15-18, we have now reached the point in time when the seventh angel sounds his trumpet, accompanied by the third woe, even though the third woe itself is not here mentioned. And so we are told at verse 11:15 that at this point in time "the kingdom of the world" is said to have become "the kingdom of our Lord and of His Christ," which is an obvious reference to God The Father and His Son; with our then being told that "He," in reference to God The Father, will now "reign forever and ever."

What this means here – especially keeping in mind what we have seen at Revelation 10:7, namely that when the seventh angel sounds, then "the mystery of God is finished" – is that what is in view here is WHAT TAKES PLACE AT THE END OF THE FOURTH AGE OF TIME, WHICH IS AT THE END OF THE THOUSAND YEAR KINGDOM REIGN OF GOD'S OWN SON, THE LORD JESUS CHRIST, over the present earth, as He now hands the kingdom He has been ruling over for the 1000 year duration of the fourth age of time to God His Father, as God has disclosed to us at 1 Corinthians 15:24-28, where we read, "[24] then *comes* the end, when He hands over the kingdom to the God and Father, when He has abolished all rule and all authority and power. [25] For He must reign until He has put all His enemies under His feet. [26] The last enemy that will be abolished is death. [27] For HE HAS PUT ALL THINGS IN SUBJECTION UNDER HIS FEET. But when He says, "All things are put in subjection," it is evident that He is excepted who put all things in subjection to Him. [28] When all things are subjected to Him, then the Son Himself also will be subjected to the One who subjected all things to Him, so that God may be all in all."

That it is God The Father Who is in view here at verse 11:15 is confirmed to us if we look at what was said at Revelation 11:17, namely "O Lord God, The Almighty, Who are and Who were, because You have taken Your great power AND BEGUN TO REIGN," and compare this to what was said back at Revelation1:4, with part of verse 1:5, and verse 1:8, where we read, "[4] John to the seven churches that are in Asia: Grace to you and peace, from Him who is and who was and who is to come, and from the seven Spirits who are before His throne, [5] and from Jesus Christ, the faithful witness... [8] I am the Alpha and the Omega," says the Lord God, "who is and who was and who is to come, the Almighty." In these verses we clearly see that God The Father is in view as "The Lord God... The Almighty" and as "Him who is and who was and who is to come," further noting verse 1:5 that God's Son, The Lord Jesus Christ, is mentioned separately.

And what is also very, very important to see here is that at Revelation 11:17, because the moment for God The Father to begin to reign has now arrived, which is after the fourth and final age of time, as before noted, we now read, "Lord God, The Almighty, Who are and who were," as past tense and now no longer saying "Who is to come," for now the time to reign has come!

Then we are told at Revelation 11:18 that "the nations were enraged, and Your wrath came," which we are to note is again past tense and would here be speaking of Revelation 20:7-10, immediately after the fourth age of a thousand year duration, where we see the final uprising of the nations against God in time being put down.

Then we are also told at verse 11:18 that "the time came for the dead to be judged," which is the event that follows Revelation 20:7-10, which is God's final judgment of Revelation 20:11-15, when all the unbelieving dead of time are now raised from the dead to stand before God to be judged by Him. This also accords with 1 Corinthians 15:26, where we are told that "the last enemy that will be abolished is death," which is now seen being abolished as all the unbelieving dead of the four ages of time are raised to life again in order to face God at the final judgment, just as the marking of time is about to end and the eternal state is about to begin.

Then the last statement of Revelation 11:18, namely, "and to destroy those who destroy the earth," goes with God's dealings with the unbelievers of time earlier at verse 11:18, namely where we read, "and the time came for the dead to be judged," for that is when all unbelievers of time, including all the fallen angels, are cast into the lake of fire by God, which is eternal hell, away from His Presence forever!

Then we note that verse 11:18 goes on with what occurs next, which is that the time has now come to reward all believers of time in the new heaven and new earth of Revelation 21:1-4, while all the unbelievers of time are now said to be destroyed, with our needing to note here that the word "destroy" does not mean to 'annihilate,' or to 'put out of existence;' but rather, the meaning here is simply that all unbelievers now lose forever all possibility of spiritual well-being, when they are cast from God's Presence forever, remaining for all eternity in conscious torment in the lake of fire, which is eternal hell, due to refusing to believe in God's Son, The Lord Jesus Christ, during their stay on earth, therefore having forfeited the forgiveness of sins from God and eternal life with Him!

Let us note what God says at 2 Peter 3:7 at this point, where we read, "But by His word the present heavens and earth are being reserved for fire, kept for the day of judgment and destruction of ungodly men." Therefore, it is important to keep in mind that the events of Revelation 11:15-18 parallel those of Revelation 20:7 to 21:4!

And we should not fail to notice here, in reading Revelation 11:15-18, that we are told that John sees a scene in Heaven, which means he is in Heaven, while at the end of Revelation 11:14, he was on earth, which is further proof that Revelation 11:15-18 occurs at the end of time, after the fourth age of time, and not at the end of the seven years remaining of the second age of time, as was the case with Revelation 11:14. And now, we can return to 1 Corinthians 15:52 now knowing that "the last trumpet" occurs at the end of the fourth age of time, and just before the eternal state begins, and also being aware of the events that take place at that time.

And so, we next read at 1 Corinthians 15:52, "the dead will be raised imperishable and we will be changed." What is in view here, as earlier noted, is the believers of the fourth age of time experiencing their part in the first resurrection, which is the fourth and last stage of it. For once these believers have been raised from the dead, as those who will have died during the fourth age and are here being referred to as "the dead will be raised;" and once all those believers of the fourth age who are still be alive at that time are translated; with both groups having their bodies changed from physical to spiritual bodies, which is what the word "imperishable" and "we will be changed" refers to here, including having had their sinful nature removed from the soul as that transformation takes place, then God will have raised in resurrection all believers of the four ages of time by this point!

Then we note that at verse 15:53, God simply states that the first resurrection, which relates to the believers of the four ages of time, has now been completed, when He states here, adding notes in brackets as a help, "For this perishable (physical human body) must put on (in resurrection) the imperishable (in reference to a spiritual body), and this mortal (body, which is now subject to aging and physical death) must put on (in resurrection) immortality" (which is now a spiritual body that will now live on forever and forever).

And before we go any further here, it is critical that we grasp here that AT NO TIME, either here at 1 Corinthians 15:51 to 57 or at Revelation 11:15-18, HAVE WE SEEN THE MENTION OF GOD'S SON, THE LORD JESUS CHIRST, APPEARING TO REMOVE THE BELIEVERS FROM THE EARTH! And the reason that we have not is due to the fact that these passages refer to the end of the fourth age of time, as when God has the fourth and last stage of the first resurrection in view, as when He now brings the believers of the fourth age to Heaven, without the mention of God's Son, since the two stages of the second coming of God's Son will have taken place a long time before this!

Then when God goes on to say at 1 Corinthians 15:54, "But when this perishable will have put on the imperishable, and this mortal will have put on immortality, then will come about the saying that is written, "Death is swallowed up in victory," we will have now reached the end of time, which includes the last judgment of God at Revelation 20:11-15, which is when all the unbelievers of time are all raised by God together to stand before Him at that last judgment!

And when that occurs, then verse 15:54 will have been realized, in that at this point all believers of time and all unbelievers of time "will have put on the imperishable," in that all will now be in a spiritual body to last forever," and all will likewise "have put on immortality," in that no human being will ever be subject to death ever again! And that is why the saying that is written (at Isaiah 25:8) will now become reality, "Death is swallowed up in victory," as what God will have accomplished as part of His plan of the ages!

We will now be at the end of time at this point, when all believers of time will now be with God on the new earth of Revelation 21:1-4, while all the unbelievers of time will now be in the lake of fire, which is eternal hell, which is this present earth having been engulfed with the fire of hell burning below the surface of this present earth since the time the devil and some angels sinned against God (noting Deuteronomy 32:22 with 2 Peter 3:7,10 and Matthew 25:41), with this burning earth now cast away from God's Presence to never be seen or thought of again by us as believers!

And so, once all believers of time have been changed into new spiritual bodies for the eternal state and no longer subject to death, and once this has also occurred for all unbelievers of time, then it is obvious that "death is swallowed up in victory," that is, it is obvious that death has been undone or reversed for all humanity! This is what we have also seen from 1 Corinthians 15:24-26 earlier, noting this again here to refresh our memories, with notes added in brackets as a help, "[24] THEN COMES THE END (of the fourth age of time, as time ends and the eternal state is about to begin), when He (God's Son) hands over the kingdom to the God and Father (that He has been ruling over during the 1000 year duration of the fourth age of time), when He (God's Son, The Lord Jesus Christ) has abolished all rule and all authority and power. [25] For He (God's Son) must reign until He has put all His enemies under His feet (which occurs during the fourth age of time). [26] THE LAST ENEMY THAT WILL BE ABOLISHED IS DEATH."

In this passage, "the end" in view is the end of time, just before the creation of the new heaven and new earth, and the beginning of the eternal state in view at Revelation 21:1-4. The "reign" in view is that of the 1000 year Kingdom reign of God's own Son, The Lord Jesus Christ, during the fourth age of time, after which, "He hands over the kingdom to the God and Father," after having "abolished all rule and authority and power," in reference to what The Lord Jesus does immediately at the close of the fourth age, as we see at Revelation 20:7-10, with the "last enemy to be abolished is death" then being the events described here at 1 Corinthians 15:51-54 now taking place, namely the bodies of the believers of the fourth age of time being changed from perishable to imperishable and from mortal to immortal, either through a resurrection from the dead or a translation; while for all unbelievers of all four ages of time they all undergo a resurrection from the dead, since all will have died (noting Hebrews 9:27), before facing God at the last judgment of time (Revelation 20:11-15), after which they are all cast from God's Presence forever, along with this earth, which will have now become eternal hell.

We then note that the apostle Paul is led of God to say at 1 Corinthians 15:55 in light of all this, "[55] O death, where is your victory? O death, where is your sting?," which is God's translation of what He had stated before at Hosea 13:14, for now death has no victory, as all human beings ever born into this world are now resurrected in new spiritual bodies to last forever, whether believers or unbelievers. This therefore means that the sting of death, in terms of its power over human lives, has now been broken by God forever, noting here what we read at Hebrews 2:14,15, "[14] Therefore, since the children share in flesh and blood, He Himself (God's own Son) likewise also partook of the same, that through death He might render powerless him who had the power of death, that is, the devil, [15] and might free (through His own resurrection to begin with, followed by the first resurrection for all believers) those who through fear of death were subject to slavery all their lives."

Then God concludes this passage, relating to "the mystery" of verse 15:51, by now saying at verses 15:56,57, "[56] The sting of death is SIN, and the power of sin is THE LAW; [57] but thanks be to God, who gives us the victory through our Lord Jesus Christ." Here we have the mention of what stood against all humanity since the time of Adam, which was SIN, AND DEATH DUE TO SIN (noting Romans 5:12)), and THE LAW OF GOD, which was spiritual and good, but which we could not obey in our sinful state apart from God (noting Romans 7:7-24) and only made human beings aware of what sin was in God's sight (noting Romans 3:20; 4:15; 5:20; 7:7).

However, the good news, as the apostle Paul goes on to say here at verse 15:57, is "but THANKS BE TO GOD, WHO GIVES US THE VICTORY THROUGH OUR LORD JESUS CHRIST. We can indeed praise and thank God that He had a solution to the human race's dilemma, which He first made known at Genesis 3:15 in promising His own dear Son, as coming to earth one day, as born of a woman, and then kept adding to that truth throughout the Old Testament until His precious Son did appear in human flesh on earth (noting John 1:1,2,14,18) to deal with sin, death, the devil, and this world system; while fully obeying God's Law on our behalf (noting Romans 5:19; 8:2-4).

And so, all believers of time will stand at the end of time and say, "thanks be to God, Who gives us the victory through our Lord Jesus Christ," for we further need to see here that the victory over sin, death, and the law, which is mentioned here at verse 15:56, was indeed won by our precious Lord Jesus Christ!

For when The Lord Jesus Christ died at the cross of Calvary the physical death that was the penalty for the sins of the whole human race, in that all humanity's sins committed in time were there laid upon our precious Lord Jesus on the cross (noting 1 Peter 2:24), so that when God's Son in human flesh was subsequently buried, HE PUT AWAY OUR SINS FROM GOD'S SIGHT FOREVER!. Then on the third day, after the death of our precious Lord Jesus Christ at the cross, God The Father raised His Son from the grave to show that His sacrifice for sins made on our behalf had been accepted of Him (noting Hebrews 9:11-14)). And with the subsequent resurrection from the dead the third day of our Lord Jesus Christ, we have the firstfruits of the first resurrection, seen at 1 Corinthians 15:20-26, whereby DEATH WAS ALSO REMOVED FROM GOD'S SIGHT FOREVER, through the subsequent resurrection from the dead of all believers and unbelievers before time ends, as we have seen here from 1 Corinthians 15:51-54!

And with the coming of The Holy Spirit to indwell believers at salvation, and with now having God's own eternal and righteous life to live by, all believers are now enabled to do what we could not do in our own strength while under the law (before salvation)! Therefore, we see that all who experience salvation in time do indeed experience victory over sin, death, and the law (noting Romans 7:4-6; Galatians 5:16-18), that being a victory won for all believers by God's own and precious Son, The Lord Jesus Christ! And what can any believer say to this, who has received God's love, mercy, and grace in salvation, except praise, honor, and glory be to God, both now and forevermore! Amen, amen, and amen!

And so, as we see here, as we conclude our detailed look at 1 Corinthians 15:51-57, this passage does NOT refer to the rapture of the church of this present third age, but rather has God disclosing truth relating to the believers of the fourth age experiencing their part in the first resurrection, while also pointing to the resurrection of all unbelievers of time also, so that as time ends and eternity begins, God will have done away with both sin and death forever and ever!

To God alone be all praise, honor, and glory, with thanksgiving, both now and forevermore! Amen, amen, and amen.

ADDENDUM A

/ The four ages of time

What is important to know when reading God's word, the Bible, is that God has divided time into four ages. And since God's word covers all of time, then all of God's word, the Bible, can be subdivided along the lines of these four ages. But before noting what these four ages are, we need to also be aware that in each of the four ages of time, God uses the believers of that age as His vessels. In other words, God is accomplishing His work on earth through the believers of each age of time.

And what is also important to keep in mind in regards to this is that although God starts each age with believers, before long the number of unbelievers in each age outnumbers the number of believers. In other words, one characteristic of each age of time is that there is a believing remnant among a mass of unbelievers, with these believers in each age being those whom God preserves for Himself and through whom God works to accomplish His purposes in each age through time.

And so, in the first age of time God worked through Adam and his believing descendants as His vessels to accomplish His will on earth, which age covers the first eleven chapters of Genesis. What this means is that they were the believers who willingly served Him out of love for Him. In other words, this was the believing line of descent, or the believing remnant, through which God worked out His will.

Then when we begin Genesis 12, we see God take one believer, Abraham, and out of that one man's descendants through the line of Isaac, and then through the line of Jacob, God makes a nation, which is Israel. And again, we need to see that only the believing line of descent within the nation of Israel was the remnant through which God worked to accomplish His will. What this means is that not all those who were of the nation of Israel were believers. In fact, the majority were unbelievers. Therefore, in the second age of time, which goes from Genesis 12 to the end of Malachi in the Old Testament, and includes the gospel accounts of Matthew, Mark, Luke, and John, plus Acts 1 and Revelation 6 to 19 in the New Testament, God works out His will in time through the believers of the nation of Israel, which is again a small number compared to the total number.

And here we need to pause for a moment and mention something else before going on to consider the third age of time, and this is the fact of representation. What this means is that in the first age of time, we have Adam and Eve as our first parents, who were but representative of all people on earth. In other words, God knew that what this one couple did, any other couple would have done the same thing, since God knows that once sin entered His perfect and sinless creation, we all would have the same sinful nature as human beings.

Then the same is true in regards to the nation of Israel in the second age of time, in that God knew that what this one nation did, any other nation on earth would likewise have done had it been chosen by God as a representative nation. So when God set out to make the one nation of Israel, He started out with just believers. But when the nation of Israel came into existence later, only a believing remnant within the nation were believers. Now since the nation of Israel was but representative of all the nations, then God knew that if He had chosen any other nation on earth, He would find that only a believing remnant would ever become believers to serve Him willingly out of love for Him out of a mass of unbelievers, who would not in any of those nations. In other words, no other human being would have acted any differently than our first parents, and likewise, no other nation would have acted any differently than the nation of Israel did. This means that all human beings and all nations are likewise guilty before God!

What also needs to be mentioned here as we now go on to look at the third age of time, is that the first two ages basically relate to the time period covered by the Old Testament, which means that the third and fourth ages of time must be covered by the New Testament portion of God's word, the Bible. And let us recall that in the first age, God worked through the believers of that age, beginning with Adam, while in the second age of time, God works through the believers of the nation of Israel, beginning with Abraham. So as we come to the third age of time, which goes from Acts 2 to the end of Revelation 5 in God's word, the Bible, we have God working through the believers of earth, whom God calls "the church."

What this means then is that in this third age of time, which we are presently still in, God is accomplishing His will through all the believers of earth, with God now not looking at any specific nation in particular. In other words, during the present third age of time, also known as 'the church age,' the nation of Israel, although being supernaturally preserved by God, is still just the same as any other nation on earth, having a believing remnant among a majority of unbelievers.

Then in the fourth age of time, which is basically covered by Revelation 20 to 22 in the New Testament, although mentioned often in prophecy in various portions of the Old Testament, we have God working through the believers of that age, but now with much greater variation. In other words, during the fourth age of time God works through the believers of every nation on earth still in their natural bodies, and also through the believers of the first three ages of time, who would have experienced their part in the first resurrection relating to believers and who are now in their resurrected bodies! This is covered in much greater detail in my book, "An Introduction To The New World That Is Coming Upon The Earth," which focuses on this fourth age of time. If there are any readers who are not sure of what is meant by the first and second resurrection and the fact of people serving God in their new resurrected bodies in the future, please see my book, "Have You Ever Wondered What Happens After Death?"

Before leaving this Addendum, it is also important to be aware that the Old Testament portion of God's word, the Bible, contains 39 books, which deal with the beginning of all things in God's plan of the ages, while the New Testament portion of God's word, the Bible, contains 27 books, which deal with the consummation of all things in God's eternal plan, which God is outworking through the four ages of time.

Also of great value is to know that the second age of time is not completed until AFTER the completion of the present third age of time. In other words, there are seven years remaining in the second age of time dealing with the nation of Israel, which is why this nation is being supernaturally preserved by God during this present third age, simply because God is not yet finished outworking His plan of the ages through that nation. These seven years remaining is a time of God's judgment against all unbelievers of earth and is approximately covered by Revelation 6:1 to Revelation 19:21 in God's word, although also mentioned often in prophecy in the Bible.

What also needs to be mentioned and is important to remember is that the reason God has a series of ages in time is in order to show us just how sinful the human race is and just how incapable it is of doing good, in terms of pleasing God on its own apart from God. What is meant here is that God's revelation of Himself increases as time progresses, so that those living in the fourth age of time as compared to the first age of time will have a far greater knowledge of God. In other words, as each age progresses, God makes it easier and easier for human beings on earth to come to know Him and to serve Him out of love for Him. For example, in the first two ages, God's precious Son had not yet come to earth, so that He was represented only through types, such as the animal sacrifices and offerings, and in prophecy. Human beings at that time also only had the Old Testament as light to guide them.

But by the time we reach the fourth age of time, God's precious Son will not only have come from Heaven to earth bodily, but will actually be on earth reigning over the nations as King. Please note what God says at Isaiah 11:9 in part, as just one example, "...For the earth will be full of the knowledge of the Lord as the waters cover the sea." What this means then is that when God's final judgment of time comes, relating to all the unbelievers of time (noting Revelations 20:11-15), then none of these unbelievers of time will be able to stand before God and give any excuse for their sin of unbelief, in having personally and freely rejected God's offer of salvation found in His own precious Son, The Lord Jesus Christ. And so, each succeeding age adds to mankind's culpability before a Holy and altogether Righteous God, so that in the end "every mouth may be closed and all the world may become accountable to God" (noting Romans 3:19 in part).

ADDENDUM B

/ The two comings from Heaven to earth of God's precious Son, our Lord Jesus Christ

Another very important truth to know here is that God's word, the Bible, mentions two comings of God's precious Son, The Lord Jesus Christ, from Heaven to earth. His first coming from Heaven to earth was for the purpose of taking on a body like ours, only in the innocence of Adam and as born of a virgin so as not to incur our sinful nature, and then after living thirty-three and half years on earth carrying out only the will of God His Father in absolute sinlessness out of love for Him, was given over into the hands of unbelievers to be put to death on a cross, before being buried, then resurrected from the dead the third day. And of course, His death was not due to anything God's precious Son, The Lord Jesus Christ, had ever done wrong, but rather was to pay the penalty due our sins, which was death, in order that God might have a basis by which to forgive the sins of those who believe in Him.

Then the second coming of God's precious Son is to be seen as being in two stages. The first stage of His second coming is at the end of this present third age of time, and is for the purpose of bringing to Heaven all believers of earth before God's judgment falls on the unbelievers of the earth, thereby bringing the present third age to a close. God has this first stage in view especially at 1 Thessalonians 4:14-17, although also mentioned in many portions of the New Testament.

Then the second stage of the second coming of God's precious Son, The Lord Jesus Christ, occurs at the end of the seven years of God's judgment, which will end the second age of time. God's precious Son would now be coming for one last battle against God's foes, as led by the devil, before establishing His reign on earth as King during the fourth age of time. This is again disclosed by God in many portions of God's word in the New Testament, but especially in passages such as Matthew 24 and Revelation 19:11-21.

ADDENDUM C

/ God's resurrection program through the four ages of time

What will be important for us to notice about this Addendum is that we not only have THE TWO COMINGS from Heaven to earth of God's Son, The Lord Jesus Christ, here in view; but we also have THE FOUR STAGES OF THE FIRST RESURRECTION, relating only to the believers of time, also in view! And in looking at God's resurrection program, relating to believers of time, it will be shown that there is ONE STAGE FOR EACH AGE OF TIME, so that God resurrects ALL the believers at one time AT THE END of each of those ages! And this is how we know that God has indeed divided time into FOUR AGES! This will be a somewhat extended, but will prove very worthwhile for the reader!

Grasping the fact that God indeed has a resurrection program in time, which begins with His Son

To begin with, let us notice that God indeed has a resurrection program in time, which, as can be expected, begins with His Son, The Lord Jesus Christ, noting here what God's Son told His disciples at Matthew 17:9,22,23 while on earth at His first coming from Heaven to earth, "[9] As they were coming down from the mountain, Jesus commanded them, saying, "Tell the vision to no one until the Son of Man has RISEN FROM THE DEAD... [22] And while they were gathering together in Galilee, Jesus said to them, "The Son of

Man is going to be delivered into the hands of men; [23] and they will kill Him, and HE WILL BE RAISED ON THE THIRD DAY." And they were deeply grieved."

This same truth can also be seen from God's gospel message that He has made known to us regarding His own dear Son, The Lord Jesus Christ. where God attests to this in a concise statement at 1 Corinthians 15:3,4, where we read, "[3] For I delivered to you as of first importance what I also received, that Christ died for our sins according to the Scriptures, [4] and that He was buried, and that HE WAS RAISED ON THE THIRD DAY according to the Scriptures…"

So what God means by a 'resurrection,' which He here makes known by what happened to His own Son is that after He died at the cross, He was buried, and then the third day, God The Father raised Him from the dead, so that He was now alive. Then forty days later, as we see from Acts 1:1-11, God's Son ascended to Heaven again, back to where He was before His first coming to earth, which is at The Father's right Hand, as where He still is today!

Grasping the fact that God's resurrection program also includes both believers and unbelievers

What should also be noticed is that Gods' resurrection program in time also includes both believers and unbelievers! This is clear from God's word, noting first of all what God tells us at John 5:28,29, "[28] Do not marvel at this; for an hour is coming, in which all who are in the tombs will hear His voice, [29] and will come forth; those who did the good deeds to A RESURRECTION OF LIFE (believers), those who committed the evil deeds to A RESURRECTION OF JUDGMENT (unbelievers)," and secondly, also seen from what God tells us at Acts 24:15, adding verse 14 for context, "[14] But this I admit to you, that according to the Way which they call a sect I do serve the God of our fathers, believing everything that is in accordance with the Law and that is written in the Prophets; [15] having a hope in God, which these men cherish themselves, that THERE SHALL CERTAINLY BE A RESURRECTION OF BOTH THE RIGHTEOUS AND THE WICKED."

Looking now at God's key passage where He makes known the four stages of His resurrection program in time

We are now at the place where we can look at God's key passage of His word, where He makes known the four stages of His resurrection program in time, which is at 1 Corinthians 15:20-26, where we read, "[20] But now Christ has been raised from the dead, the first fruits of those who are asleep. [21] For since by a man came death, by a man also came the resurrection of the dead. [22] For as in Adam all die, so also in Christ all will be made alive. [23] But each in his own order: Christ the first fruits, after that those who are Christ's at His coming, [24] then comes the end, when He hands over the kingdom to the God and Father, when He has abolished all rule and all authority and power. [25] For He must reign until He has put all His enemies under His feet. [26] The last enemy that will be abolished is death."

What we will now do is go through this passage in detail and point out each stage of God's resurrection program in time as we go along. And so, at verse 20 to 22 here, God begins by first making it clear that because His Son has been raised from the dead, then all believers of time will most assuredly also be raised from the dead! It is only starting at verse 23 that God begins to point out the four stages of His resurrection program in time.

So God begins at verse 20 here by telling us, as the believers of the present third age, that His Son "has been raised from the dead" already, as what has been noted above, so that for us in the present third age, this is an event which has taken place in the past. Then God continues and says that His Son's resurrection from the dead took place as "the first fruits of those who are asleep," meaning as the first of the harvest of precious souls that is coming from believers of time, who would also have died as His Son has, but who will in the future experience a resurrection from the dead also, same as His Son did, since God's Son is only "the first fruits" to God of the harvest to come!

Then at verse 21, God goes on and says that "since by a man came death," in reference here to Adam at the beginning

115

of time, for the consequence of Adam's sin was death, which then spread to the whole of the human race, since Adam is the first man and the one from whom the whole of the human race is descended, noting what God tells us about the sin of Adam and its resulting consequence of death at Romans 5:12, "Therefore, just as through one man (Adam) sin entered into the world, and death through sin, and so death spread to all men, because all sinned."

And what God means by "all sinned" here is that the whole human race, like Adam, is born into this world innocent, but at the age of accountability, which is the age known only to God when a young child first learns right from wrong and chooses the wrong, therefore personally sinning against God and becoming personally accountable to God for that sin. It is "because all sinned" that no parents ever have to teach their children how to sin, for that comes naturally from one's sinful nature that one has now incurred at the age of accountability!

And then coming back to 1 Corinthians 15:21 above, we then note that after saying that "since by a man (Adam) came death," as we have just discussed above, God goes on and now adds, "by a man (God's Son) also came the resurrection from the dead," with God specifically pointing out here that one of the principal reasons for His Son coming from Heaven to earth at His first coming was to undo the devil's work.

In other words, as we see at Genesis 3, it was the devil, who is there seen as the serpent, who led Adam and Eve into sin, which, as we have seen above, resulted in the human race not only becoming sinners at the age of accountability, but also all subject to death as a result of sinning against God! So God sent His Son, born of a virgin (Matthew 1:18-25; Hebrews 10:5), Who after being born into this world in the innocence of Adam, carried out His Father's will in sinless perfection for thirty-three and a half years before dying on the cross as the penalty due the sins of the human race, then being buried before being raised from the dead the third day, and then ascending to His Father's side forty days later, where He still is today!

What this means then is that in His Son, The Lord Jesus Christ, dying for the sins of the human race at the cross, God has a basis for forgiving sin, when a sinner believes that Christ's death was to pay the penalty of one's sins committed against God since the age of accountability. And then in God's Son being raised from the dead the third day, then God has a basis for giving eternal life to every sinner who believes that God's Son has been raised from the dead and is now alive forevermore, since it is through His Son that God grants that eternal life!

So we see then that God undoes the devil's work of bringing sin and death to the human race by bringing the forgiveness of sins and eternal life to every sinner who believes the good news (the gospel, noting 1 Corinthians 15:1-4) that God has made known regarding His Son, The Lord Jesus Christ. And not only that, but since God's Son was raised from the dead, and He is the "first fruits," then that means that every believer of time will likewise be raised from the dead also before time ends!

This is exactly what God brings into focus for us at verse 22, especially in the second part, when He there says, "For as in Adam all die, so also in Christ all will be made alive," speaking here of all believers of time, who experience a physical death in time, they too will experience a resurrection from the dead, just like His Son did, just by virtue of now being believers through having believed in God's Son to receive from God the forgiveness of sins and His eternal life!

And before we go on to look at 1 Corinthians 15:23, where God starts to make known the four stages of His resurrection program in time, there are three very important truths that we need to grasp here from what we have just seen from verses 20 to 22. The first truth is that once God's Son, The Lord Jesus Christ, was raised from the dead, and then entered Heaven, He was no longer subject to physical death, which means the same is also true for all believers of all ages of time! Therefore, the critical truth to see here is that God's Son was now THE FIRSTBORN OF A NEW CREATION OF GOD, which further means that every believer who also

117

experiences God's resurrection from the dead is also part of that new creation of God! So what would be beneficial, and what is now highly recommended, if one ha not already done so, is for the reader to turn to Addendum D, also at the back of the book and read, "God's new creation in time," before resuming here.

Then the second important truth that we need to be aware of here, before we look at verse 23, is that God's resurrection program that God will now disclose for us, in relation to believers of time, is what God refers to as THE FIRST RESURRECTION in His word. So let us note Revelation 20:6, where God mentions that first resurrection, "Blessed and holy is the one who has a part IN THE FIRST RESURRECTION; over these the second death has no power, but they will be priests of God and of Christ and will reign with Him for a thousand years."

What should be obvious here, from God's use of the words "blessed" and "holy," is that God only has believers in view as those who partake of that "first resurrection." And what this further means then is that the four stages of God's resurrection program that we will now be looking at beginning at 1 Corinthians 15:23 are what constitutes that first resurrection! In other words, when all the believers of the four ages of time have all been resurrected from the dead, of those that will have died physically, then God's first resurrection will have been completed!

The third very important truth that we need to grasp here relates to the statement at verse 22 that "in Christ all will be made alive," which is the fact that, as we will see, the term "made alive" refers not just to believers who have died physically, and are now resurrected from the dead, but also includes those believers who may still be alive physically, who now undergo a TRANSLATION into new spiritual bodies without going through physical death at all. So for them the "made alive," which is one word in the original Greek, refers to one going from living physical life in a human body temporarily to going on to live a spiritual life in a new spiritual body, which is now forever! This is also an important truth for us to remember as we go on.

And so, in now coming to 1 Corinthians 15:23 from our passage quoted above, we see that God here states, adding verse 22 again for context, "[22] For as in Adam all die, so also in Christ all will be made alive. [23] But each in his own order: Christ the first fruits, after that those who are Christ's at His coming..." So we see that after saying at the end of verse 22 that "in Christ all will be made alive," regarding all believers of time who will have died physically and those still alive physically who will have been translated, He then goes on at verse 23 to point out that there is an "order" to God's resurrection program that God regards as the first resurrection. In other words, it is to be done in an orderly arrangement, which we would be justified in identifying as 'STAGES' here. What this means then is that God's order or first stage of His resurrection program relating to the believers of time God identifies as, "Christ the first fruits."

But what is critical to see here is that at verse 20, when God was specifically focusing on His Son, The Lord Jesus Christ, He there said, "But now Christ has been raised from the dead, THE FIRST FRUITS of those who are asleep," where we saw that God there meant that His Son was the first or principal part of a harvest that would later follow and include all the believers of time. However, here at verse 23, since God is speaking at the end of verse 22 of "all will be made alive," in reference to all the believers of time being raised from the dead or translated, with His then going on to give the orderly arrangement or stages of that resurrection relating to the believers of time, God now says, "Christ the first fruits," where it should be clear that the word "first fruits" – which is one word in the original Greek, that being "Aparche" – now refers to SOME BELIEVERS ALSO, and not just to God's Son alone!

What this means then is that the words "first fruits" here come from two Hebrew words in the Old Testament, that being "Reshith," meaning 'the beginning, choice, chief, or principal part,' while the other is "Bikkurim, which means 'the earliest

119

ripe of the crop.' Both Hebrew words are found in what God says at Exodus 23:19a, where we read, "You shall bring the choice (Reshith) first fruits (Bikkurim) of your soil into the house of the Lord your God."

So what this means for our present purpose here then is that at 1 Corinthians 15:23, when God says, "Christ the first fruits," God is indicating by that statement, based on what has just been said above, that at the time that God's Son was resurrected from the dead ALL the believers of an earlier age in time, which would be of the first age of time, were also raised from the dead at that time!

And if we look at Matthew 27:52,53 in God's word, for instance, this is exactly what we are told by God did occur, adding verses 50,51 for context, "[50] And Jesus cried out again with a loud voice, and yielded up His spirit. [51] And behold, the veil of the temple was torn in two from top to bottom; and the earth shook and the rocks were split. [52] The tombs were opened, and many bodies of the saints who had fallen asleep were raised; [53] and coming out of the tombs AFTER HIS RESURRECTION they entered the holy city and appeared to many."

What God is telling us here at verses 50,51,to begin with then, is that at the moment that God's Son, The Lord Jesus Christ, died at the cross, the veil in the temple in Jerusalem was torn in two, that is, the veil between the two compartments of the temple, that being the holy place from the Holy of holies, which veil spoke of the body of God's Son (noting Hebrews 9:2-5 with Hebrews 10:19,20) was now removed, indicating that believers would henceforth have direct access to God The Father through His Son, Who had now gone to Heaven in God's Presence to minister on behalf of believers (noting Hebrews 7:24-27; 8:1,2; 9:24).

Then at verses 52,53, we see that what took place "after His resurrection," that is, after God's Son had been resurrected from the dead by His Father three days later, the tombs were then opened – indicating here that wherever it was on earth that these believers had died, whom God calls "saints" here – they were now raised from the dead and entered the city of

Jerusalem in Israel and appeared to many, who would themselves have been believers. And please note that God says here that they "appeared to many," in order to indicate to us that they were now visible, even though in a new spiritual body to last forever. So just as God's Son was raised from the dead with a body that was now spiritual, but still visible, so too with believers, when raised from the dead by God, they too now have spiritual bodies that will last forever, in terms of never being subject to death again, but which are to be seen as visible!

So what is important to grasp here is that since what we read here at Matthew 27:50-53 occurred in the second age of time (noting again Addendum A here, if need be), then this means that those resurrected from the dead with The Lord Jesus Christ here, as the "first fruits" of verse 15:23, are the believers of the first age of time here experiencing their part in the first resurrection, which would here be the first stage of it at the time of the resurrection from the dead of God's own dear Son!

There is another passage, which we need to make mention of here, which also speaks of these same believers from the first age here in view at verses 52,53, who are the "first fruits" of verse 23, which is to now note what God tells us at Ephesians 4:8-10, where we read – and please note that the "He" throughout is a reference to God's Son, The Lord Jesus Christ at the time of His death, burial, resurrection from the dead, and ascension back to Heaven again; while the brackets at verses 9,10 are part of the Bible text – "[8] Therefore it says, "WHEN HE ASCENDED ON HIGH, HE LED CAPTIVE A HOST OF CAPTIVES, and He gave gifts to men." [9] (Now this expression, "He ascended," what does it mean except that He also had descended into the lower parts of the earth? [10] He who descended is Himself also He who ascended far above all the heavens, so that He might fill all things.)"

So, what God is making known at verse 8 here is that when His Son ascended back to Heaven again, forty days after His resurrection from the dead (noting Acts 1:1-3) "He led captive a host of captives," in reference to the believers of the first age of time, who had died physically, now freed from death forever in resurrection from the dead and now ascending to Heaven with God's Son, The Lord Jesus Christ, in His ascension! In other words, just like a conqueror in war has his spoils, so too with God's Son, His death, burial, and resurrection from the dead secured for the believers of a past age freedom from bondage to sin and death forever! And so, we see again here that these being led to Heaven by God's Son at the time of His ascension forty days after His resurrection are the "first fruits" of 1 Corinthians 15:23, which is the first stage of God's FIRST resurrection program!

If we then continue at 1 Corinthians 15:23, we note that after saying in the first part of the verse, "But each in his own order: Christ the first fruits," God then goes on and says, "AFTER THAT those who are Christ's AT HIS COMING." In other words, the next stage then in God's resurrection program, relating to the believers of time, is "at His coming." And since we know for sure that the first stage of God's first resurrection program took place at the time of the death, burial, resurrection from the dead and ascension back to Heaven again of His dear Son, The Lord Jesus Christ, which was at HIS FIRST COMING from Heaven to earth, this therefore means that what God has in view here when He says "at His coming" is the SECOND COMING from Heaven to earth of God's Son!

And now it is critical for us to grasp that the second coming of God's Son from Heaven to earth actually takes place in TWO STAGES! In other words, God speaks of His Son returning to earth again in the future not once, but twice, which we will see to be seven years apart!

So to begin with here, let us note some passages of God's word where God speaks of the FIRST STAGE OF THE SECOND COMING of His Son, The Lord Jesus Christ, from Heaven to earth, noting what we read at 1 Thessalonians 4:13-18, with some notes added in brackets as a help, "[13] But we do not want you (believers) to be uninformed, brethren, about those (believers) who are asleep (have died physically), so that you will not grieve as do the rest (unbelievers) who have no hope (because they do not know God). [14] For if we believe that Jesus died and rose again, even so God will bring with Him those who have fallen asleep in Jesus (that is, when He comes again, He will bring with Him the spirit of these believers who died as believers). [15] For this we say to you by the word of the Lord, that WE WHO ARE ALIVE UNTIL THE COMING OF THE LORD, will not precede those who have fallen asleep (that is, will not be translated before those who have died as believers are raised from the dead). [16] For the Lord Himself will descend from heaven (but remain in the clouds above, as we see at verse 17) with a shout, with the voice of the archangel and with the trumpet of God, and THE DEAD IN CHRIST WILL RISE FIRST. [17] THEN WE WHO ARE ALIVE AND REMAIN WILL BE CAUGHT UP TOGETHER WITH THEM IN THE CLOUDS TO MEET THE LORD IN THE AIR, and so we shall always be with the Lord (from that point onward). [18] Therefore comfort one another with these words."

And so, we see here that at the FIRST STAGE OF THE SECOND COMING OF GOD'S SON FROM HEAVEN TO EARTH, the believers of the present third age that God has here in view will be "made alive," in that God's Son will descend from Heaven in the clouds and remain just above the earth, then He will call forth all the believers, both those whose bodies are still in the graves on earth and whose souls and spirits are now returning, along with all the believers that are still alive, as these will never have seen physical death; in that all of these will now have their bodies transformed into spiritual bodies to last forever (noting 1 Corinthians 15:42-44), all having their sinful nature removed from the soul and now being brought into God's Presence forever!

Then we see that at 2 Thessalonians 2:1, God again speaks of that FIRST STAGE of His Son's SECOND COMING, where we read, "Now we request you, brethren, with regard to the coming of our Lord Jesus Christ and our gathering together to Him..." The "gathering together with Him" here is at "the coming of our Lord Jesus Christ," is the same event that we have just seen mentioned above at 1 Thessalonians

4:14-17, which is THE FIRST STAGE OF THE SECOND COMING of God's Son from Heaven to earth!

As we continue, let us now note where God speaks of the SECOND STAGE OF THE SECOND COMING of His Son from Heaven to earth, which is now to be seen as being approximately seven years later, with God's Son now coming directly to the earth, and not just in the clouds above the earth, as at the first stage of His second coming. And so, let us start by looking at Matthew 24:1-3, where we read, "[1] Jesus came out from the temple and was going away when His disciples came up to point out the temple buildings to Him. [2] And He said to them, "Do you not see all these things? Truly I say to you, not one stone here will be left upon another, which will not be torn down." [3] As He was sitting on the Mount of Olives, the disciples came to Him privately, saying, "Tell us, when will these things happen, and what will be the sign of YOUR COMING, and OF THE END OF THE AGE?"

What needs to be observed from this passage is that this conversation between God's Son and His disciples was taking place during the FIRST COMING from Heaven to earth of God's Son, which was at during the second age of time. And here we have His disciples ask two questions, the first relating to "when" that "coming" would be; and the second relating to "what" will be the "sign" that will accompany that second coming, which we are told will then bring that second age they were then in to an end.

What is critical to see here then is that THE AGE IN WHICH GOD'S SON HAD HIS FIRST COMING FROM HEAVEN TO EARTH WILL NOT END UNTIL THE SECOND STAGE OF THE SECOND COMING OF GOD'S SON TAKES PLACE! What this means then is that the age God's Son was in when on earth at His first coming (which was the second age of time, noting again Addendum A, if need be), He will still be in the same age at the second stage of His second coming from Heaven to earth! And what this further means is that in relation to us living on earth now, we have the first coming of God's Son from Heaven to earth about 2000 years ago and the second stage of His second coming at some point in time yet future from our own day!

Then we are to note that in answer to the question of "when" that second coming would be, which as mentioned will be the 'second stage' of it, we are to note from what God's Son goes on to say from Matthew 24:4-28 that until the coming of God's Son, there will be a time of "tribulation" (verse 9) and then a time of "great tribulation" (verse 21) with all that is being said here being in the context of the nation of Israel.

In other words, we are to observe that throughout here, the nation of Israel is in view. Not only were they on the temple mount in Jerusalem in Israel when this conversation of verses 24:1-3 took place, but God's Son Himself had come to earth as born of a virgin of the nation of Israel (Matthew 1:1-25 with Romans 9:3-5) and His disciples were all of the nation of Israel! So what we can say about the second age is that it has both the first coming and the second stage of the second coming of God's Son from Heaven to earth and that it has the nation of Israel as its central focus!

Then what is then very important to observe is that God's Son also answers the disciples second question here, relating to "what will be the sign of your coming and of the end of the age" at verse 3, noting now what God's Son tells the disciples at Matthew 24:29-31, "[29] BUT IMMEDIATELY AFTER THE TRIBULATION OF THOSE DAYS the sun will be darkened, and the moon will not give its light, and the stars will fall from the sky, and the powers of the heavens will be shaken. [30] And then the sign of the Son of Man will appear in the sky, and THEN ALL THE TRIBES (that is, all the people) OF THE EARTH will mourn, and they WILL SEE THE SON OF MAN COMING ON THE CLOUDS OF THE SKY WITH POWER AND GREAT GLORY. [31] And He will send forth His angels with a great trumpet and they will gather together His elect from the four winds, from one end of the sky to the other."

What is important to realize here is that this second stage of the second coming of God's Son from Heaven to earth now takes place with God's Son RETURNING DIRECTLY TO

125

THE EARTH, and not just in the clouds above the earth, as was the case with the first stage of His second coming!

This fact is made clear from what God tells us at Luke 24, Acts 1, and Zechariah 14. So let us note first what God tells us at Luke 24:50,51, "[50] And He led them out as far as BETHANY, and He lifted up His hands and blessed them. [51] While He was blessing them, He parted from them and was carried up into heaven." We are to note that since "Bethany" was a village about two miles east from Jerusalem (noting John 11:18), and since Bethany was on the eastern slope of Mount Olivet, then that is where God's Son actually ascended from back to Heaven at the time of His first coming from Heaven to earth.

This is actually confirmed to us from what we read from Acts 1:9-12, where we have the same ascension from earth to Heaven of God's Son, but now with a little more detail, where the second stage of His second coming is also mentioned, [9] And after He (God's Son) had said these things, He was lifted up while they were looking on, and a cloud received Him out of their sight. [10] And as they were gazing intently into the sky while He was going, behold, two men in white clothing (that is, two unfallen angels in male human form) stood beside them. [11] They also said, "Men of Galilee, why do you stand looking into the sky? This Jesus, who has been taken up from you into heaven, WILL COME IN JUST THE SAME WAY AS YOU HAVE WATCHED HIM GO INTO HEAVEN. [12] Then they returned TO JERUSALEM FROM THE MOUNT CALLED OLIVET, which is near Jerusalem, a Sabbath day's journey away."

Then from Zechariah 14:4, we see that God had prophesied that when His Son returned to earth from Heaven, which is again at the second stage of His second coming, then it will be on Mount Olivet, just east of Jerusalem, which is the exact spot that we see from Acts 1:11,12 that God's Son ascended from at the time of His first coming and now is coming back to at the time of the second stage of His second coming! So let us read what God tells us at Zechariah 14:4, "In that day His feet will stand on the Mount of Olives, which is in front of

Jerusalem on the east; and the Mount of Olives will be split in its middle from east to west by a very large valley, so that half of the mountain will move toward the north and the other half toward the south." The "Mount of Olives" mentioned here is the "Mount Olivet" of Acts 11:12 above.

So it is clear from the passages we have looked at here, relating to the second coming of God's Son from Heaven to earth at some time in the future, that the first and second stages of that second coming are two separate events, not only based on the fact that the one is said to be in the clouds above the earth, while the other is directly to the earth, but also by the SIGNS that accompany both stages of that second coming.

For instance, at 1 Thessalonians 4:16, which is during the first stage of the second coming of God's Son, we read, "For the Lord Himself will descend from heaven with a shout, with the voice of the archangel and with the trumpet of God, and the dead in Christ will rise first;" while at Matthew 24:29, which is at the second stage of the second coming of God's Son, we now read of totally different events taking place as signs of that coming, "But immediately after the tribulation of those days the sun will be darkened, and the moon will not give its light, and the stars will fall from the sky, and the powers of the heavens will be shaken."

And so, what this means then relating to 1 Corinthians 15:23 and the stages of God's resurrection program in time relating to all believers is that the first stage of the second coming of God's Son from Heaven to earth is the SECOND STAGE of God's resurrection program, which we will see takes place at the end of the present third age of time; while the second stage of the second coming from Heaven to earth of God's Son is the THIRD STAGE of God's resurrection program in time, which will be at the end of the fourth age of time, after the 1000 year reign of God's Son will have ended! So let us keep that in mind as we now return to our passage at 1 Corinthians 15:20-26 that we have been looking at here.

Then at 1 Corinthians 15:24-26, we see that God then introduces the fourth stage, which is the last stage of His resurrection program relating to believers of time, when He there says (which we repeat here again to refresh our memories), "[24] THEN COMES THE END, when He hands over the kingdom to the God and Father, when He has abolished all rule and all authority and power. [25] For He must reign until He has put all His enemies under His feet. [26] THE LAST ENEMY TO BE ABOLISHED IS DEATH."

So let us note that "the end" that God has in view at verse 24 here is the end of time, which therefore means that this is indeed the last stage of God's resurrection program relating to the believers of time. And the key thought for our present purpose of looking at the fourth stage here is what we see at verse 26, when God talks of abolishing death, which is just before time comes to an end. And based on what we have already noted, the question here is: How does God go about abolishing death? If you said to yourself, "Through a resurrection," then that would be entirely correct, for that is what God has in view here.

And so, since death is abolished by God resurrecting from the dead all believers and unbelievers alike before time ends, this then is what we see occurring in this fourth stage of God's resurrection program, in that God first resurrects all the believers of the fourth age on earth before the end of time, and then God has the resurrection from the dead of all the unbelievers of time take place all at once, immediately after and also before time ends. So whereas the resurrection from the dead of believers in time takes place in four stages, as we are showing in this Addendum, nevertheless, the resurrection of ALL unbelievers of time takes place ALL AT ONCE at the end of time, which is at the last judgment of time of Revelation 20:11-15!

As to the fourth stage of God's resurrection program relating to believers of time, we are to note that God gives us a fairly detailed look at that fourth stage at 1 Corinthians 15:51-57, where we read, again adding notes in brackets as a help, "[51] Behold, I tell you a mystery; we will not all sleep (that is, not all believers will die physically), but we will all be changed (whether one has died physically or whether one is still alive when this fourth stage of God's resurrection program comes, all believers alike will inherit a spiritual body to now enter God's Presence), [52] in a moment, in the twinkling of an eye, at the last trumpet; for the trumpet will sound, and the dead will be raised imperishable, and we will be changed (going from the physical body of this realm to the spiritual body of God's realm, where all is spiritual). [53] For this perishable must put on the imperishable, and this mortal must put on immortality. [54] But when this perishable will have put on the imperishable, and this mortal will have put on immortality, then will come about the saying that is written, "Death is swallowed up in victory. [55] O death, where is your victory? O death, where is your sting?" [56] The sting of death is sin, and the power of sin is the law; [57] but thanks be to God, who gives us the victory through our Lord Jesus Christ."

So what we see God saying here is that during this fourth stage of God's resurrection program relating to believers of time, the believers that are yet alive and those that will have died at that time will be changed by God in an instant, thereby receiving a spiritual body to enter God's Presence in Heaven, simply because that is a spiritual place (noting again 1 Corinthians 15:42-44). What this means then is that when that occurs, then physical death relating to the believers of time will be no more, as now God will have changed from physical bodies of earth into spiritual bodies for Heaven every believer of time, whether one had died or one was still alive when that occurred!

And so to summarize here: By the time we reach the end of time, God's FIRST RESURRECTION will have been completed by God, in that He will have completed the four stages of His resurrection program relating to believers of time, which are in view in that first resurrection, and all believers of time will now have a new spiritual body to last forever in God's Presence!

And as God points out at verse 57 above, God's resurrection program relating to the believers of time is only possible due to what God's Son has done on behalf of a sinful human race, which, as earlier indicated, was secured through His death to pay the penalty due the sins of mankind, His burial to put those sins away from God's sight forever, and then Himself being raised from the dead the third day by God His Father, so as to be alive forevermore, for it is through His Son, as alive forevermore, by The Holy Spirit, that God gives eternal life to those who believe in His Son for salvation, which then secures for each one a part in God's first resurrection in time that we have been looking at!

Then as to the resurrection of UNBELIEVERS of time, also in view at verse 15:54 above, we are now to see that this takes place at the last judgment of God, which God mentions at Revelation 20:11-15, when ALL UNBELIEVERS OF TIME, WHO WILL HAVE ALL DIED PHYSICALLY BY THIS POINT, BAR NONE (noting Hebrews 9:27), WILL NOW ALL BE RAISED FROM THE DEAD BY GOD, as we there read, again adding notes in brackets as a help, "[11] Then I saw a great white throne and Him (God The Father in His Son) who sat upon it, from whose presence earth and heaven fled away, and no place was found for them. [12] And I saw the dead (all the unbelievers of time), the great and the small, standing before the throne, and books were opened; and another book was opened, which is the book of life; and the dead were judged from the things which were written in the books, according to their deeds. [13] And the sea gave up the dead which were in it, and death and Hades gave up the dead which were in them (that is, wherever the dead bodies of the unbelievers of time might be, in the grave, under the earth, or even in the sea); and they were judged (all unbelievers of time all at once), every one of them according to their deeds. [14] Then death and Hades were thrown into the lake of fire (literal hell). This is the second death, the lake of fire. [15] And if anyone's name was not found written in the book of life, he was thrown into the lake of fire."

So as we see here, as now relating to all the unbelievers of time, before God's Son hands over the kingdom of Heaven that He will have been ruling over for a thousand years by this point (noting 1 Corinthians 15:24 with Revelation 20:4), and as part of putting all His enemies under His feet (as we see at 1 Corinthians 15:25), all unbelievers of time will now

130

be judged by Him in this final judgment of time, before each one is cast into the lake of fire, which is literal hell, which we are to see will actually be this earth and its heavens, which now turns into that lake of fire, noting what God says at 2 Peter 3:7, "But by His word the present heavens and earth are being reserved for fire, kept for the day of judgment and destruction of ungodly men."

We should note in closing this chapter that God refers to what occurs to all unbelievers of time here as "the second death" at verse 14 above, simply because all unbelievers of time are now all raised from the dead by Him and given bodies that will now last forever, in order for death to be abolished before time ends, but also because in being cast by God into hell, which is forever alive in that place of torment, these unbelievers are now away from God's Presence forever.

So the death these unbelievers all experience during time is first a physical death, and now in being cast away from God's Presence forever, this is now a "second death," which is also to be seen as a spiritual death, in that they will be cast from God's Presence forever. Let us note again verse 11 above, "from whose (God's) presence earth and heaven fled away, and no place was found for them." Since that earth and heaven will now be literal hell, and that is where all unbelievers of time will be, then that is what God means by the "second death" at Revelation 20:14 above, in that these will now be away from God and His spiritual realm – which will also include being away from all unfallen angels and all believers of time – forever and ever.

And so, as time comes to an end, we see that God will have completed His resurrection program in time relating to all believers of time, which we have now seen is in FOUR STAGES, which constitutes what God refers to as His FIRST resurrection. What this means is that each of these stages of the first resurrection occurs at the end of each age of time. And since we have seen that there are four stages to God's resurrection first resurrection program relating to all believers of time, this then means that God has divided time, and His Word, into FOUR AGES!

ADDENDUM D

/ God's new creation in time

A very important truth to know here is that God is building a new creation through His Son in time, which consists of all believers of the four ages of time! Just as God brought about His original human creation through the first man, Adam, during the time of the first covenant; now God brings His new human creation into being through His Son, as "the last Adam" and "the second Man" (noting 1 Corinthians 15:45,47), as part of God's new covenant. So just like the first human creation that God brought into being was a physical one; we will now see that this new human creation that God is now bringing into being is a spiritual one! And now in this Addendum we will look at the fact of there being a new creation of God; then show that God's Son, The Lord Jesus Christ, is the basis for God's new creation; before closing by showing when this new creation of God begins and ends.

1) The fact of a new creation of God

First then, let us note that just as there was an original physical human creation from God in time, as is clear from what God tells us at Mark 10:6, "But from the beginning of creation, God made them male and female," then there is also a new spiritual human creation from God, noting what God tells us at 2 Corinthians 5:17, "Therefore if anyone is in Christ, he is a new creature; the old things passed away; behold, new things have come," and also at Galatians 6:15,

"For neither is circumcision anything, nor uncircumcision, but a new creation." There had to be an original human creation for there to be a new spiritual creation, and there was, as we have just seen.

2) God's Son, The Lord Jesus Christ, is to be seen as the basis for God's new human spiritual creation!

Then secondly, just as the whole of God's original creation, including humans, came into being through God's firstborn, that being His Son, The Lord Jesus Christ, as we see from Colossians 1:15-17, "[15] He (The Son of God) is the image of the invisible God, the firstborn of all creation (in terms of being first to appear on the scene, that is, in terms of The eternal Son coming forth from eternity into time, by Whom His Father then created all that came into being as part of the original creation, including human beings). [16] For by Him all things were created, both in the heavens and on earth, visible and invisible, whether thrones or dominions or rulers or authorities – all things have been created through Him and for Him. [17] He is before all things (because eternally existing), and in Him all things hold together."

So also then, the new creation of God comes into being through His firstborn, that being His precious Son, noting what God goes on to tell us at Colossians 1:18, "He (The Son of God) is also head of the body, the church; and He is the beginning (of God's new human spiritual creation), the firstborn from the dead (speaking here of the very moment of the resurrection from the dead of God's Son, The Lord Jesus Christ), so that He Himself will come to have first place in everything," from that moment on and into all eternity to come!

Another passage of God's word which we need to note here, because it also speaks of God's eternally existing Son being the firstborn of both the original physical creation and of the new spiritual creation of God is Hebrews 1:6, where we read, "And when He (God The Father) AGAIN brings the firstborn into the world, He says, "And let all the angels of God worship Him." What is very important to note is that when God says "again" here, He is saying that His own eternally-existing Son was first seen in the world at the time of the original physical creation, when God The Father created all that exists in the original creation through His Son by The Holy Spirit, as we have seen at Colossians 1:15-17 above. And then He brought His Son into the world a second time, this being at the time when He took on a body as human beings have, but born of a virgin woman in the innocence of Adam so as not to incur our sinful nature, as we see for instance at John 1:14, "And the Word became flesh, and dwelt among us, and we saw His glory, glory as of the only begotten from the Father, full of grace and truth," and also at Hebrews 10:5, "Therefore, when He (God's Son) comes into the world, He says, "Sacrifice and offering You have not desired, but a body You (God The Father) have prepared (in the womb of the virgin named Mary) for Me" (The Son of God).

3) Seeing when God's new spiritual creation through God's Son actually begins and is completed in time

And then as to the question of WHEN does God's new spiritual creation through His Son actually BEGINS and is COMPLETED in time, we need to look at what God tells us at 1 Corinthians 15:45-49, "[45] So also it is written, "The first man, Adam, became a living soul." The last Adam (speaking here of God's Son, The Lord Jesus Christ, at His first coming from Heaven to earth) became a life-giving spirit. [46] However, the spiritual is not first, but the natural; then the spiritual. [47] The first man is from the earth, earthy; the second man (in reference to God's Son) is from heaven. [48] As is the earthy, so also are those who are earthy; and as is the heavenly, so also are those who are heavenly. [49] Just as we (as believers) have borne the image of the earthy, we will also bear the image of the heavenly."

And so, we see here that God's Son, Who came from Heaven to earth to take on a human body at the time of the Incarnation, that is, at the time of His embodiment in human flesh, which is the moment God The precious Father conceived a body in the womb of Mary, while yet a virgin, is here called "the last Adam" and also "the second man" in

135

relation to God's new human spiritual creation, in contrast to the first man of the original creation, that being Adam! Then we are also told here by God that just as all human beings "have borne the image of the earthy, so will we also (as those who are believers among human beings) bear the image of the heavenly."

And in regards to this "image of the heavenly," which it is clear from the context that God's Son came to earth to bring, we must also note what God says at Romans 8:29, "For those whom He foreknew, He also predestined to become conformed to the image of His Son, so that He would be the firstborn among many brethren," where we learn that all those chosen of God in eternity past for salvation in time, who are here "those whom He foreknew," are "also predestined to become conformed to the image of His Son," which begins at the time of one's justification, when one comes to personally know God in salvation, but will not be completed until the time of one's glorification, which is when one enters God's Presence as now "spiritual," that is, where one now bears "the image of the heavenly" forever, with a body changed to a spiritual body and with the sinful nature removed from the soul.

Then another passage which needs to be noticed here is what we read at John 12:23,24, "[23] And Jesus answered them, saying, "The hour has come for the Son of Man to be glorified. [24] Truly, truly, I say to you, unless a grain of wheat falls into the earth and dies, it remains alone; but if it dies, it bears much fruit." And what The Lord Jesus Christ meant by "the hour has come for The Son of Man to be glorified," is that the time had arrived for Him to enter His Father's Presence in Heaven again at the ascension, in reference to Acts 1:9-11, which event, as we see from verse 12:24 above, could only occur after a physical death and resurrection from the dead. In other words, the physical body that The precious Father gave His Son in the womb of the virgin thirty-three years before would now die at the cross, be buried, and then be raised from the dead the third day. However, when raised from the dead the third day, it would now be as a glorified body, that is, as a body which although visible would nevertheless be spiritual, which will be so forever in His Father's Presence!

And so, the only way that believers, as those who are chosen of God for salvation, can ever be conformed to the image of God's Son, The Lord Jesus Christ, is also through physical death and glorification, that being through a resurrection from the dead, if one has died, or a translation to a spiritual body, if one has not died (noting for instance 1 Thessalonians 4:14-17 here), when one's time of glorification comes. One passage we can note here is Philippians 3:20,21, "[20] For our citizenship (as believers) is in Heaven, from which also we eagerly wait for a Savior, The Lord Jesus Christ; [21] Who will transform the body of our humble state into conformity with the body of His glory, by the exertion of the power that He has even to subject all things to Himself." When that happens, that is, the moment of our glorification, then we as believers will "bear the image of the heavenly," which God's Son, The Lord Jesus Christ, already bears and which He made possible for all believers of time!

Therefore, as to "when" the new creation begins and is completed, we can say that for God's Son, The Lord Jesus Christ, the new creation began at the moment of His Incarnation, but was not completed until the moment of His glorification, which is when He was raised from the dead the third day after His death at the cross and burial. And so, in the same way for those among human beings chosen of God for salvation, which are all those who come to know God in a personal relationship in salvation in every age of time, one becomes part of God's new creation at the moment of one's salvation, which is justification, but which is also not completed until one's glorification, when one's sinful nature is removed and one is given a new spiritual body to live forever in God's Presence!

And so to summarize, as we have been told by God at 1 Corinthians 15:46 above, namely that "the spiritual is not first, but the natural; then the spiritual," so we are to see that just as God's own Son took on our humanity as born of a virgin in the innocence of Adam, whereby God The Father eternally united His eternally existing Son with a human body provided by God, as the last Adam, to begin a new human spiritual creation, and through death, burial, and resurrection from the dead, completed that new creation as the firstborn from the dead, thereby going from the Heavenly to the earthy to the spiritual and Heavenly; then so too with human believers. We, who are the chosen of God, at the moment of one's salvation, which is justification, one who is earthy is united with God through His Son by The Holy Spirit, as the beginning of one becoming a new creation of God, which new creation is then completed at the time of one's glorification, which is when one has the sinful nature removed from the soul and receives a spiritual body for the one of flesh, thereby also going from the earthy to the spiritual and heavenly, so as to live in glory, which is in God's Presence forever!

4) Seeing a new heaven and a new earth as a new creation of God for all eternity of the new human creation of God from time!

What also needs to be observed is that just as God created the original earth, with two heavens (one seen and one unseen, the first created heaven being associated with the original earth, while the second created heaven, which is unseen, is associated with the angels) for His original human creation, then He also will create in the future a new earth for His new human spiritual creation, with its two heavens (one associated with the new earth and the other associated with the unfallen angels), as is clear from what God tells us at 2 Peter 3:13, "But according to His promise we are looking for new heavens and a new earth, in which righteousness dwells," and also at Revelation 21:1-4, "Then I saw a new heaven and a new earth; for the first heaven and the first earth passed away, and there is no longer any sea. [2] And I saw the holy city, new Jerusalem, coming down out of heaven (which is the third Heaven here, as God's eternal and uncreated abode) from God, made ready as a bride adorned for her husband. [3] And I heard a loud voice from the throne, saying, "Behold, the tabernacle of God is among men, and He will dwell among them, and they shall be His people, and God Himself will be among them, [4] and He will wipe away every tear from their eyes; and there will no longer be any death; there will no longer be any mourning, or crying, or pain; the first things have passed away."

When God says that "the first things have passed away" here, He is speaking of His original creation, which all unbelievers of time are still associated with, but which is here seen to be away from God's Presence eternally! The important information to remember here is that after the fourth age of time, we have the eternal state, which is when God creates a new heaven and new earth, which will be specifically for His new human spiritual creation of time!

"Jesus said to him, "I am the way, and the truth, and the life; no one comes to the Father but through Me."
"

John 14:6

ADDENDUM E

/ For those who may not as yet know God

Possibly you have been reading this book and have become aware of not knowing this God Who created us and gave us physical life into this world, and up to now has allowed you to live on earth. However, you do have the desire to know God in a personal way. If this is the case, then this Addendum has been written specifically for you.

And what God wants you to have in coming to know Him is the peace and joy which comes in knowing that all of your sins committed in your lifetime are forgiven and that you have eternal life with God. And so, your greatest need at the moment is to make peace with God so as to go to Heaven, which is God's eternal home. And so, this Addendum will help to bring that about by pointing you to God so as to come to faith in Him.

And as we begin, we need to note a most important promise which God makes at Romans 6:23 to all those who do not yet know Him, "For the wages of sin is death, but the free gift of God is eternal life in Christ Jesus our Lord." The good news here is that God offers you eternal life with Him as a free gift, which is to be obtained in His Son, Jesus Christ. What God does not do in this verse from the Bible is tell us 'how' to obtain that eternal life with Him.

Another verse which we can look at where God does let us know 'how' one can obtain that eternal life with Him is noting what God tells us at John 3:16, "For God so loved the world, that He gave His only begotten Son, that whoever believes in Him shall not perish, but have eternal life." Now the added truth which God makes known here is that the eternal life, which He gives to a human being as a free gift, is for those who believe in His Son.

Then the question is: What is it that I am to believe about God's Son, Jesus Christ, which will lead God to give me eternal life with Him forever? And the beauty of God is that He never leaves us guessing, especially when it comes to having a personal relationship with Him, which He desires us to have. Therefore, we should not be surprised when God gives us the answer to our question in what He tells us at 1 Corinthians 15:1-4, "[1] Now I make known to you, brethren, the gospel which I preached to you, which also you received, in which also you stand, [2] by which also you are saved, if you hold fast the word which I preached to you, unless you believed in vain. [3] For I delivered to you as of first importance what I also received, that Christ died for our sins according to the Scriptures, [4] and that He was buried, and that He was raised on the third day according to the Scriptures..."

Therefore, "the gospel," which simply means 'good news,' which God wants you to hear and believe in order to "be saved," which simply refers to you coming to know God and have eternal life with Him, is that His Son has already died for you, has already been buried, and has already been raised from the dead again the third day after His death, in order that God would have a basis by which to forgive you of all your sins, which are all against Him, and to freely give you eternal life with Him, for simply believing this message in your heart.

One thing which often prevents a person from believing the gospel at this point is not seeing oneself as a sinner before a Holy God. When we look at ourselves by our own assessment, and especially when we compare ourselves with

144

others around us, we often think of ourselves as being better than others, and so good enough to enter Heaven in our present condition. The problem with this is that it is the product of our own thinking and is not God's assessment of our situation.

God's assessment of our situation is as He tells us at Romans 3:10-12,23 in part, "[10] as it is written, "There is none righteous, not even one... [11] there is none who seeks for God [12] all have turned aside... there is none who does good, there is not even one... [23] for all have sinned and fall short of the glory of God..." Quite a different assessment of the human race from that which we as human beings often have of ourselves, is this not? But why would God have such an assessment of the whole human race? For the answer to that question, we need to be aware that God is Creator of all that exists, so that when God created the first man, Adam, at the beginning of time, God created him in innocence, meaning that Adam as first created by God neither knew good nor evil, nor was there any sin anywhere in God's original sinless creation.

However, the day came when God tested Adam with a command, saying to him in the garden of Eden here on earth, which was the perfect environment which God had for him, what we now read at Genesis 2:16,17, "[16] The Lord God commanded the man, saying, "From any tree of the garden you may eat freely; [17] but from the tree of the knowledge of good and evil you shall not eat, for in the day that you eat from it you will surely die." How important to see here that God gave Adam, who although a real person was also representative of the whole human race, the warning of the penalty of death for disobedience to His command.

Unfortunately, the day did come when Adam did partake of the forbidden tree and thereby did sin against God. The moment that happened, Adam not only became a sinner by practice, but also a sinner by nature. One thing my parents had to continually do while under their care was to restrain me from continually going the wrong way, for it seemed that of myself I could not do good, but kept going into sin. The reason this was happening is that from the age of accountability onwards, I had not only become a sinner by practice, but also a sinner by nature.

And here the age of accountability needs to be seen as being when as a young child in innocence - which moment is known only by God - one comes to learn the right from the wrong and chooses the wrong, thereby becoming personally accountable to God for one's own sin against Him, since all sin is first of all against Him. And that is why God can say at Romans 3:23 above that "all have sinned and fall short of the glory of God," because God knows that all human beings will go the way of Adam, our representative man, which is also why God can say what He does in regards to the whole of the human race at Romans 5:12, where we read, "Therefore, just as through one man (Adam) sin entered into the world, and death through sin, and so death spread to all men, because all sinned" (from the age of accountability onward). And so, we see that the whole human race is declared by God to not only be sinners by practice and by nature from the age of accountability onwards, but the whole of the human race is now subject to death! In other words, in God's sight the whole of the human race is under the judgment of the penalty of death, due to all being sinners by practice and by nature.

You will recall above, in the first verse we quoted from Romans 6:23, God did say there that "the wages of sin are death." And what God means by "death" here is not just loss of physical life, when the physical body we have dies, but also has spiritual death in mind, which is far worse! Spiritual death has its beginning when a separation takes place between a person and God at the moment one becomes a sinner at the age of accountability and ends after the final judgment of time, when God forever casts away from His Presence those who before physical death refused to believe in His Son, The Lord Jesus Christ, thereby personally forfeiting the forgiveness of their sins and eternal life with God. And now all such will pay the penalty for their own sins in hell, away from the Presence of God forever.

It is in the midst of such a hopeless situation in which the whole of the human race found itself in that God TOOK THE INITIATIVE and sent His own eternally existing Son into the world, as born of a virgin in the innocence of Adam – so as not to inherit the sinful nature passed on from generation after generation from Adam onwards through the conception of the female – so that He might be the acceptable sacrifice offered to God His Father at the cross, there bearing our sins in His body, and there dying the death due our sins! God's Son, Jesus Christ, was then buried and raised from the dead the third day, to ever be alive, for it is through Him, on the basis of what God has done for us through His Son, that God The Father forgives our sins and imparts us eternal life.

Now, by God's grace and His enablement, may you see your need of God's Son to be Your Savior from the penalty due sin, which is death, not only physical, but also spiritual. And by God's grace, may He lead you to believe in His Son, Jesus Christ, and in believing, to receive the forgiveness of your sins and eternal life with Him forever! And based on the truth just shared, the author would now like to ask you a few questions, with the answer being just between yourself and God:

When God says at Romans 3:23, "for all have sinned and fall short of the glory of God," does that include you?

When God says at Romans 5:8, "But God demonstrates His own love toward us, in that while we were yet sinners, Christ died for us," were you included in Christ's death on behalf of sinners?

And when God further says at 1 Peter 3:18 in part, "For Christ also died for sins once for all, the just for the unjust, so that He might bring us to God, having been put to death in the flesh, but made alive in the spirit," were you part of the unjust for whom Christ died?

When God says at Romans 6:23, "For the wages of sin is death, but the free gift of God is eternal life in Christ Jesus our Lord," do you want that eternal life as a free gift from God?

When God says at John 3:16, "For God so loved the world, that He gave His only begotten Son, that whoever believes in Him shall not perish, but have eternal life," do you now believe that Jesus Christ is indeed God's Son in human flesh, Who came from Heaven to this earth to die in your place, so as to save you from ever experiencing the judgment of God leading to an eternal separation from God in hell?

And when God then further says to you at Isaiah 55:6, "Seek the Lord while He may be found; call upon Him while He is near," for His further promise to you here is as we read at Romans 10:9-11,13, "[9] that if you confess with your mouth Jesus as Lord, and believe in your heart that God raised Him from the dead, you will be saved (that is, you will now enter into a personal relationship with God by faith); [10] for with the heart a person believes, resulting in righteousness (that is, in now receiving God's own righteous and eternal life to live by), and with the mouth he confesses, resulting in salvation (that is, in now receiving as a free gift the forgiveness of sins and eternal life with God). [11] For the Scripture says, "Whoever believes in Him will not be disappointed..." [13] for "Whoever will call on the name of the Lord will be saved." Will you now call upon God from your heart in your own words being mindful of your answer to each question that have just been asked?

The author's prayer for you at this point, as you now call upon God by His grace, is what we read at Romans 15:13, "Now may the God of hope fill you with all joy and peace in believing, so that you will abound in hope by the power of the Holy Spirit."

/ The next book

As this book is being published, God has given His servant the go-ahead to write another book, titled "God's Letter To The Hebrews." In case it is not the next book, the reader may want to check with the author's website to see what book has been published:

http://www.pilgrimpathwaypublications.com

If you have found this book profitable, or any other of the author's books, please feel free to let family, friends, and co-workers know about this book and the other books. The author is not on any social media sites, so he relies on God and readers to spread the word. May God bless you for doing so!

Manufactured by Amazon.ca
Bolton, ON